CHARITY ON CAMERA
IN EDWARDIAN BRISTOL

CHARITY ON CAMERA
IN EDWARDIAN BRISTOL

A PHOTOGRAPHIC SURVEY OF THE CITY PROPERTIES OF THE BRISTOL MUNICIPAL CHARITIES, 1906

KIERAN COSTELLO AND RICHARD BURLEY

DB
PUBLISHING

First published in Great Britain byThe Breedon Books Publishing Company Limited
Breedon House, 44 Friar Gate, Derby, DE1 1DA. 1999

This paperback edition published in Great Britain in 2015 by DB Publishing, an imprint of
JMD Media Ltd

ISBN 978-1-78091-515-9

Printed and bound in the UK by Copytech (UK) Ltd Peterborough

Contents

Preface 7

Introduction 8

Chapter 1   The Year 1906 10

Chapter 2   Charity 16

Chapter 3   The Properties 20

Chapter 4   Children 25

Chapter 5   The Elderly 33

The Photographs 38

Appendices 102

1) Almshouses, Annuities and Gifts administered by the Bristol Municipal Charities,
from the *Bristol Municipal Charities. Year Book 1905-1906*

2) Schedule of the Bristol Municipality Charities' properties organised by charity

Ordnance Survey maps, Central Bristol, 1903.

Bibliography 114

ACKNOWLEDGEMENTS

This project could not have been completed without the assistance of a number of people. First and foremost, the authors' thanks are owing to the Trustees of the Bristol Municipal Charities who gave permission for their photographs to be published. The officers of the Charities have also been most generous in giving time to make the records available, and for providing advice about their operation of their organisation. We would particularly like to thank Richard Hawkins, Peggy Cherrington, Michelle Hooper and Stephen Barrow for help in this respect. Moira Martin from the University of the West of England read an early draft of the manuscript and gave us the benefit of her expertise on the social history of Bristol at this time, although any remaining errors of judgement or fact are ours. John Williams, the City Archivist, has been very supportive of the project and Anton Rippon at Breedon Books has been a model publisher. Finally, we must thank our respective partners for their patience Barbara Costello and Jane Brock, for not only putting up with a project that has caused disruption to domestic and social routines, but also for reading the final drafts and making helpful suggestions.

Preface

Photographs of old Bristol abound, but it is rare to find an extensive yet integral collection taken at a specific period in time. But that is what we have in this unique set belonging to the Bristol Municipal Charities which depicts the Edwardian Bristol of 1906; this is the reason we have felt able to expand the text to place the photographs in context, by examining the visual image they present and providing a background to the period to which they relate.

In order to prevent repetition of the full title, we have used various shorthand mechanisms throughout the book. The Bristol Municipal Charities is referred to as the BMC (more properly B.M.C.), the Municipal Charities or the Charities, all with capitals. Where charity is indicated with a lower case 'c', this refers to the concept of charity in general.

At the time of writing, the records of the BMC are split between the Bristol Record Office (BRO) and the Charities although there is a likelihood that the majority of archive material will eventually all be housed in the BRO. As a rule of thumb, the pre-municipal reform records up to 1835 are in the Bristol Record Office; documents post-1836 are still with the Charities except school admission records and some letter books. The Bristol Record Office reference to the combined collection is BRO/33041/ BMC, whilst the specific reference for the photographic collection that forms the core of this book is BRO/33041/BMC / 12/1. When BMC documents are referred to in the footnotes without a BRO prefix, this signifies that the document is still in the custody of the Charities at the time of writing.

Introduction

Around Easter 1906, a photographer wandered the streets of Bristol's inner city undertaking a photographic survey of the Bristol Municipal Charities' urban properties. Whether he walked, or more likely, used a bicycle adapted with carrying gear for the equipment, his unwitting testimony was to leave us, at the end of the twentieth century, with a unique record of the topography of the Edwardian city centre.[1] The photographer was possibly from Edward Brightman and Company of 39 Colston Street, St Augustine's, as they had been given permission to undertake a similar survey of the city properties in 1902. The evidence is inconclusive, however, as there is no record of payment to a photographer in any of the account books of the Charities for the relevant period. Two years later, in 1904, the BMC appointed a new surveyor of the city properties, Frank Wills, so it may be that this portfolio was commissioned and paid for by him as an *aide memoire* in dealing with a fairly substantial property estate.

Our ability to place this collection in time rests in clues which crop up in the photographs themselves; a meeting of the Religious Tract Society on Monday, 9 April and a newspaper poster referring to the San Francisco earthquake whose tremors hit that city on Wednesday, 18 April 1906. There are posters advertising Easter train excursions, too. The streets themselves seem relatively empty of traffic, as if the photographer had chosen a quiet time in the morning before the day's activities had fully started, or at the weekend when work traffic had lessened. The boys in quite a few of the photographs seem to be dressed in their Sunday best, too. The conclusion appears to be that, although this is a collection put together for the purpose of making a visual record of all the BMC properties, its composition took a few excursions to complete; note, for example,

the evidence for different weather conditions that prevail from one photograph to another.

Although taking photographs had become easier because of technological progress which improved the quality of portable camera equipment during the late Victorian period, making a photographic record was still a fairly cumbersome operation. Our cameraman probably used a field camera, which folded to form a narrow box for transporting. The camera was extremely light, weighing no more than two kilogrammes, and was placed on a tripod, each leg of which was clipped into stays on the underside of the camera itself. All in all, it took about five minutes to set the equipment up, assuming there were no problems in framing the view to be taken. Including travelling time, the whole set of prints must have taken over a week of solid work to complete. The clarity of this process is such that, when the originals are viewed through a magnifying lens, it is possible, for example, to see the suspicious face of a cat as it sits, disturbed from cleaning itself, at the back of the inner courtyard of one of the almshouses (photograph no. 9). The collection is very important, therefore, for drawing out aspects of the lives of Bristol's citizens (including the cats) as they went about their business, although no reproduction can be as good as the originals in highlighting these micro-details. Even more important, is that of all Bristol's individual photographic surveys for the Victorian and Edwardian periods, it is the largest and most comprehensive for showing what the centre of the city looked like at any one moment in time.

The BMC were created in 1836 as one outcome of municipal government reforms in the previous year, and so are the oldest of Britain's municipal charities. The Charities' antecedents, though, stretch back to the late Middle Ages.[2] The BMC survives to this day and

1 This photographic survey survives amongst the documentary collections of the Bristol Municipal Charities and is kept at Bristol Record Office (BRO/33041/BMC/12/1). There are 94 prints in total, mounted within two contemporary photograph albums. Each print measures 15 x 11cm and there is a duplicate pair of albums, with the addition of a few photographs, in the vaults of the Charities.

2 The standard reference work on the development of Bristol's charities is the two volume tome W. Manchee, *Bristol Charities*, 1831

has its headquarters in Orchard Street. It continues to administer the revenue from its various property holdings in Bristol and surrounding counties, using the proceeds for the same charitable purposes it has always done. Whilst our focus is on its urban portfolio in 1906, the BMC was also a country landholder, particularly in south Gloucestershire. Since the value of its rural property fluctuated in line with the fate of the agricultural economy, its city properties created a relatively stable income which, over time, profited from rising urban land values. That is not to say that urban property was a foolproof investment. Depressions in property prices, with subsequent knock-on effects in the rental value, are a feature of the Victorian period and a couple of the exemplars in the chapter on the properties indicates that the rental value of shop premises went down by about 10% between 1900 and 1906. City properties also needed more money and time spent on them than agricultural land. One of the potentially fascinating investigations which this book cannot cover, because it entails an analysis of financial records over a much longer period of time, is how the Bristol Municipal Charities managed its estates in order to provide the maximum income for its charitable duties, and the extent to which this management reflected best practice. Charities usually have the luxury of only needing to spend what they generate in income, but what they manage to achieve always depends on how they anticipate, or react to, market conditions.

The BMC was an endowed charity and, in general, endowed charity is poorly studied in comparison to other forms of welfare provision.[3] This is even more the case for the twentieth century and a short analysis like this cannot do full justice to the deficiency. This apparent lack of interest is counteracted by extensive research on the Poor Law system and welfare intervention by the state, particularly on the period after, and including, Gladstone's Liberal administration in the 1880s. Endowed charities, however, can be particularly rich in the range and quantity of records that they create (and the BMC is especially well provided for in this respect) all of which

document a host of financial, architectural and social issues. For example, the plan books of the properties are detailed enough to view the configuration of rooms in working-class housing in the mid nineteenth century, and the outline of original rooms within buildings which have Medieval and Tudor origins. There are records of individuals, many of them working-class people, from which direct or indirect evidence of poverty and personal circumstances become apparent. This is in contrast to the useful, but impersonal data provided by Poor Law statistics.

The main text in the book focuses on the background to issues that were current at this period, as the first chapter in particular will begin to bring out. Subsequent chapters deal with the mechanics of how the Bristol Municipal Charities went about their business, and analyse facets of the lives of the two main groups of people who benefitted from their benevolent provision - children and the elderly.

The photographs are arranged alphabetically by street in the main part of the book. This more or less mirrors how they are arranged within the two albums which contain the originals; this in turn follows the sequence in the BMC's property schedules. The accompanying text to each print provides information about how the properties you see in the photograph were used and, where appropriate, details about the history of the structure(s). The whole, therefore, is intended to place the role of the Brtistol Municipal Charities in Bristol around 1906 into some sort of context, as well as highlight how its documentary and photographic records can be used as evidence of the city's appearance at this time. Because there are two routes through the book, some minor elements of detail are repeated in both sections as they are relevant to the material being discussed at that point. Finally, the appendices list the remit of the separate charities that formed the BMC and a schedule of property under ownership; we hope this will give the reader a better spatial understanding as to where the property holdings of each of the composite charities was.

3 See chapter 2

CHAPTER 1

The Year 1906

Progress?

Anyone trying to analyse Britain during the initial few years of this century is faced with a dilemma: are we dealing with an historical period that is essentially nineteenth century and, therefore, Victorian in character, or is it a period that exhibits features which we take to be recognisably twentieth century in their manifestation like the presence of the phone or motor car, for example? These photographs were taken at the cross-roads of this change. The death of Victoria from an apoplectic stroke in 1901 was a psychological watershed which, to one commentator, signalled that 'the great Victorian age is at an end. …It will mean great changes in the world',[1] but not all reflections on her personality were as complimentary:

The queen came across, her horse drawn carriage, across Bristol Bridge, and I remember saying, 'Is that our queen? That wizened old so-and-so?' I said, 'I thought she was a grand old lady,' course this tiny little wizened lady in the corner of the carriage. Quite disappointed to think that was our queen cos you see that beautiful statue in College Green of a majestic woman, well I didn't see anything of the sort.[2]

Analysis today can still follow the cult of personality in determining historical turning points, but most social historians would look for underlying causes to set their parameters. The period from 1870 to 1914, with an internal phase that lasted from 1890 to the start of the First World War, is a block of historical time which seems to have integrity in this respect.[3] All ages exhibit facets of both change and continuity and no place better expresses this paradox than Bristol. The sheer dynamism of social life and expansion of the city, from 1870 to the outbreak of war in 1914, is a complex and rich field of study to analyse. 'We have parted with many ancient features …but progress is ruthless and in a variety of cases the old must give way to the new' suggested one writer on Bristol's outward appearance.[4] Other observers of the scene at the time were aware of this physical change, combining as it did a sense of nostalgia for the great Victorian era that had passed, yet proud of the concept of change, especially change in the physical environment which had cleansed Bristol of its accretion of squalor built up over the centuries, and swept away in paroxysms of smashing and widening by that quintessential agent of Victorian urban reform — the Corporation's Sanitary and Improvement Committee.

At the turn of the century, young people in particular were encouraged in the belief that they had inherited the benefits of the previous generation's successful attempts at cleansing the Augean stable:

A marvellous change has come over the appearance of the city during the recent years. Forty years ago, the narrow, twisting, irregular streets, and the antiquated, inconvenient buildings of Bristol, made it one of the queerest and most unhandsome of large towns. Visitors now

1 The poet Wilfed Blunt entering the demise of the Queen in his diary 31 December 1900 quoted in the preface of Simon Nowell-Smith, ed., *Edwardian England 1901-1914*, 1964
2 *Bristol People's Oral History Project*, Recording no. 39: transcript, p. 6, referring to Queen Victoria's visit to the city in 1897
3 For a current overview, see Chapter 1 in Jose Harris, *Private Lives, Public Spirit: Britain 1870-1914*, 1994
4 *The Bristol Observer*, 21 July 1906

declare it one of the finest English homes of commerce. Few, perhaps too few, of its ancient buildings have been spared in the march of progress, but the worst slums have entirely disappeared.[5]

At first glance the photographs reflect this analysis. On the whole, things look neat and tidy, but we are looking at main street frontages most of the time, and it was not entirely true to say that the worst slums had entirely disappeared. They lurked behind the main streets, out of camera shot, and were owned by landlords less scrupulous than the BMC. The courts and alleys we see in the pictures are all neat and tidy as the Charities kept their property in relatively good condition and tended to dispose of problem structures.

Most Bristolians of the time, though, would probably have agreed with W.L. Dowding's suggestion (quoted above) that their city was placed at the end of a march of progress, of which rebuilding was regarded as one of the most important achievements. *Modern Progress*, which included coverage of the opening of the Central Free Library and the National Nautical School at Portishead in 1906, was the summative chapter in his history book for teenagers; it was preceded by chapters on Bristol's great and the good: Edmund Burke, Robert Southey, and those denizens of mid nineteenth century charity and education, George Muller and Mary Carpenter. Colston was there too, but no mention of any slavery connection. Other observers felt more at home with the notion of the new century as marking a new start or period of reinvention, but also hinted at regret for that which had been lost, and so show that nostalgia for the past is clearly not just a current trend.[6] That feeling of anguish for lost fabric is also found in the writings of an anonymous commentator who mused on how he never walked along Temple or Thomas

Streets, two thoroughfares which are reflected in the BMC portfolio:

without imaginings of what the city must have been like two or three centuries ago. In Thomas Street several houses remain which are of "mature age" … I suppose one looks at the "remnants" of another time with greater interest because it is the best way of reading the characters of those times. And in Thomas Street the old inns remind you of the days when there were no railways, and when bicycles and motors had not been thought of… Stabling accommodation and a large yard were requisites of the inn a century ago, but so much has happened in the interval to alter our notions of the conditions of life.[7]

The existence of books and newspapers like these reflects another facet of that age — literacy. There were over 2500 newspapers in the British Isles by 1906, in addition to magazines and a wide choice of books. The national press had been revitalised by the founding of the *Daily Mail* (1896) and The *Daily Mirror* (1903), two newspapers which created the concept of the popular press. Provincial newspapers were important, too, and Bristol had eight.[8]

Dimensions

Capturing the city as they do at one point in time, these photographs reflect the outcome of this 'improvement' and it is probably true to say that if anyone was to walk our photographer's route today they would be more familiar with his world than a resident of one of the Bristol Municipal Charities' almshouses in 1906 would be with the Bristol of his or her childhood in the early Victorian period.

Of course, the physical landscape in these photographs gives no clue at all as to how big Bristol

5 W.L. Dowding, *The Story of Bristol: A Brief History For Young Citizens*, 1906

6 See Stanley Hutton, *Bristol and its Famous Associations,* 1907 and George Frederick Stone, *Bristol As It Was — And As It Is. A Record of Fifty Years' Progress*, 1909. This substantial tome was a reprint, with additions, of articles which had previously appeared in issues of the *Bristol Evening News*

7 *Bye-the-Bye* column, *The Bristol Observer*, 10 March 1906

8 The collections in the Bristol Central Library contain *Bristol Evening News, Bristol Evening Times and Echo, Bristol Guardian, Bristol Mercury and Daily Post, Bristol Observer, Bristol Times and Mirror* and *Clifton Chronicle*

was by 1906. If these photographs had been taken 40 years earlier they could truly be said to have represented the City and County of Bristol. By 1906 they exemplify what contemporaries called the 'old city' or 'ancient city', forming the new concept of an inner city that had been created as a result of extensions in Bristol's administrative boundaries. Even in 1891, the city and county contained the modest total of 4538 acres; by 1906 it had risen to 17,289. A population of 222,049 in 1891 had grown to 339,042 by 1901, and to 357,048 by the time the next Census enumeration came round in 1911, an increase of 5.3% over the decade. A good deal of what can be taken for growth was down to absorbing already existing suburban areas. In 1906 the 'old city' comprised an area of 810 acres. Its population of about 55,000 in 1891 had by 1906 fallen to 41,000. This decline in population in the inner city, against a rising trend in the suburbs, was a much longer-term phenomenon that had been going on since at least the 1820s.

From such statistics, Bristol's Medical Officer of Health could demonstrate that population density had dramatically fallen from nearly 50 to 21 people per acre, but these figures mask the fact that the benefit of space and fresh air was the prerogative of the middle and skilled working classes who lived away from the city centre. The Corporation was particularly proud of its parks and open spaces (750 acres in all including the Downs), but there were no parks in the old city; in fact there was hardly a blade of grass. Whilst Westbury on Trym had the generous density of two people per acre and Stapleton nine, Clifton had 30, St George (an already populated area which had come into Bristol in the boundary change of 1897) 35; the density in the inner city was 50. Nor do these figures do justice to the pockets of overcrowding that average statistics hide. In St Paul, in 1891, the density was a staggering 130 followed closely by St James at 115. The benchmark for ensuring healthy living, according to the authors of a report into Bristol's housing conditions, was 25, so severe overcrowding had not only an effect upon living conditions, but also on health.[9]

Housing and Health

Bristol Hovels: The Report of the Bristol Housing Reform Committee in 1907 is the most important of contemporary documents in attempting to open the debate as to the lack of quality housing stock and poor health amongst inhabitants in the city centre.[10] They took issue with the city Medical Officer's assertion that statutory overcrowding was not common in Bristol. Whilst technically this was the case,

Ward	Houses registered as inhabited	Houses registered as uninhabited but occupied	Houses registered as uninhabited but unoccupied	Houses under construction	Population
Bristol	911	553	65	2	5938
Redcliffe	2400	239	168	8	14,216
St Augustine's	1012	141	84	-	7020
St James	1007	163	65	1	6588
St Michael	1998	107	137	1	11,860
St Paul	2306	173	68	3	14,207
St Philip north	4367	119	187	28	25,431
St Philip south	3811	83	96	-	20,674

Table of inhabitation in central Bristol: source: Table 9, Gloucesterhire, 1901 census

9 See A. Cooke, *Bristol Hovels: The Report of the Bristol Housing Reform Committee*, 1907, p. 6
10 *ibid.*

the comparison with the statutory definition then in force did nothing to assuage critics who believed that the resulting, complacent attitude by the city's Health Committee prevented sufficient attention being devoted to areas where the problem was acute.[11]

The catalyst for the report was a major fire in Broadmead in 1907, which, if it had got out of control, would have destroyed all of the houses in the area. The originator of the Reform Committee, Frank Sheppard, based his criticisms on the lack of progress in the Health Committee's officers' attempts at reducing disease and death. Specifically, the Reform Committee's tramping of the inner city revealed problems; many buildings were old and dirty; back-to-back houses still existed and many dwellings lacked a separate water supply. Lack of ventilation, high rents, lack of consideration for tenants whose houses were pulled down for improvements or extension of commercial premises also added to the problems.[12] In trying to analyse what was actully happening, one has to balance one attitude against the other; between the laissez-faire attitude of the Council to problems that undoubtedly existed, compared to an unquantifiable list of complaints by the Bristol Housing Reform Committee, although, to be fair to them, their survey was only intended as a swift sweep of the centre to provide specific case studies and ensure continuation of the debate rather than to provide a comprehensive, statistical analysis. One house was so bad that 'the sky could be seen through the roof, and there were large holes in the floors of the two upper rooms. When the wife was last confined, in stepping out of bed her leg went through the floor, and was seen by her husband in the room below'. In the central district they examined 31 houses in eight separate streets and courts where the rents of the houses ranged from 2s. 6d. a week for two rooms, to 4s. 6d. a week for six rooms (this compares to the 10 shillings

per week charged on rent for the Charities' substantial houses in Orchard Street or an average rent of four shillings per week for one of their cottages in Broad's Court). In terms of overcrowding, the worst case witnessed a family of 10 occupying three rooms.[13]

On a related issue they criticised the lack of municipal control over the tramway system and the knock-on effects this had on creating a viable housing policy — 'provision of cheap and speedy means of access must go hand-in-hand with the provision of suitable dwellings'.[14] The poor quality of the Bristol Tramway Company's workmen's service led to unacceptable overcrowding on the St George route. 'The tramway is as necessary to a modern city as were the streets to those of a bygone generation: it is in fact nothing more than the extension of a street, and as such, should be maintained by the city for the use of the citizens'.[15] Their economic argument for civic control compared the savings that accrued to the ratepayers in boroughs such as West Ham, Salford, Sheffield, Liverpool, Glasgow, Hull, Leeds and Manchester where there was municipal control. In many respects, this argument summed up the inability of Bristol's local government to take effective action to take control of essential services in order to remedy need. Whilst London and other cities had excellent examples of initiatives to improve housing through refurbishment programmes as undertaken by the likes of Octavia Hill, the 5% philanthropy movement or municipal flats, Bristol's main contribution was the provision of one or two municipal lodging houses which only gave temporary accommodation and were used mainly by people new to the city.

The range in quality of inner city housing is reflected in the photographs, too, as the condition of some buildings are in a practically ruinous state whilst others are clean and well kept. One aspect of people's lives that is not so apparent from photo-

11 Clearance of courts was being tackled by the end of the century. In 1890 there were 320 courts housing 2000 people which had dropped to 165 courts housing 1000 people by 1912. See Madge Dresser, *People's Housing in Bristol 1870-1939* in Bristol Broadsides, *Bristol's Other History*, p. 133
12 *Bristol Hovels*, p.10: see also in general Dresser, *op. cit.*
13 *Bristol Hovels*, pp. 11-12
14 *op. cit.*, p.14
15 *ibid.*

graphic evidence, however, but which very much related to living conditions, was the matter of health.

Dr D.S. Davies, the Medical Officer of Health for Bristol, despite opposition from socialist reformers and perhaps a natural pride at improvements which he and his officers had achieved, was as conscientious a medical officer as the city could have hoped for. He was, in fact, only the second officer to hold the post since it started in 1861 (the first office holder was his father). Davies was a statistical man, collecting data on a multitude of issues that fell within his brief. Principally, it was zymotic diseases (a disease caused by multiplication of germs from an external source) that were uppermost in his mind. For 1906 the number of deaths for each disease in this category was: small pox (0), measles (140), whooping cough (102), diptheria (79), typhoid (21), influenza (47), diarrhœa(213); asiatic cholera (0) and scarlet fever (27). This is put into perspective, however, when the number of deaths from a cause as simple as contaminated milk totalled 435 (although the resulting mortality must have included a number of cases of diarrhœa and typhoid) and 50 cases of mortality put down to keeping animals or domestic pets. Of the zymotic diseases, small pox, a highly contagious disease, was the one that caused most worry owing to an outbreak in the south of the city. In consequence, 'Inspectors were detailed to visit and watch all contacts, numbering nearly 3,000. These Inspectors did nothing else for three months, viz.: from the end of February to the first week in June, when the disease was mastered, although the work of general inspection had to suffer in consequence.'[16]

Because of the strict attention to control on matters which affected the health of the population — constant inspection of lodging houses, tenements, slaughter houses, factories and workshops, drains, offensive trades and smoke nuisances, Bristol's health had showed steady improvement over time. Of the 28 largest towns in Britain and Ireland, only Hull had a lower zymotic death rate than Bristol

in 1906, and it was a figure that had regularly and steadily declined since 1891.[17]

Local Government

Expansion in boundaries also meant expansion in local government remit. Despite the fact that Bristol went against the trend by having its water, gas and transport systems in private hands, it still had control of, and, therefore, committees devoted to: Estates and General Purposes (the Corporation was a huge landowner and the annual rental income provided £20,000 to the city's coffers); Watch; Docks; Education; Distress (set up in response to the 1905 Unemployed Workmen Act); New Streets; Museum and Art Gallery; Pilotage; the Downs; Health; Electricity; Sanitary and Improvement; Baths; Libraries; Disease of Animals; a Visiting Committee of the Lunatic Asylum; Burial Board; Finance, and the ultimate for the Local Authority that has almost everything — a Selection Committee on Committees. Despite the costs of administration, its plethora of committees and the inevitable sub-committees meant it went about its business with a zeal and precision for detail that was the hallmark of local government at the turn of the century. So, for example, under powers given to it by the Shop Hours Act 1904, the Council effected an order limiting the opening hours of hairdressers, barbers and shaving shops.[18] Every three months the Sanitary and Improvement Committee had the pleasure of listening to Benjamin Kitt, the Gas Examiner, presenting his report. He was responsible for public lighting, and of his brood of 8,786 gas lights, 5816 were in the 'old area' and 2970 in the 'extended area'. New expenditure went to the extended areas. Of the 58 new gas lamps provided in the financial year from April 1905 to March 1906, only 3 were destined for the inner city. In all, the Corporation spent £3953 3s. 3d. on gas in that council year (the vast majority of which went on street lighting) using 44,208,330 cubic feet in the process.[19]

16 *Bristol Medical Officer of Health's Report, 1906*, p. 102

17 *op. cit.*, table 4

18 *Proceedings of the Council*, vol. 24: 9/11/1905 — 23/10/1906, p. 70

19 *op. cit.*, p. 255

The Council itself consisted of 22 aldermen and 66 councillors. Of the 21 new councillors elected in November 1905, four were styled as 'gentlemen'. There were also two 'esquires', three grocers, two estate agents (one of whom also acted as an undertaker), a veterinary surgeon, builder, goldsmith, carrier, corn merchant, wine merchant, stockbroker and draper with a telegraphist and a bootmaker making up the rest of the new contingent, so only one or two could truly be said to represent working class occupations. However, the balance was probably representative at a local level of the emerging socialist vote that was to be apparent in the 1905 national election which took place in the following month.[20]

The General Election of December 1905 was, without doubt, the most significant political event around this time and an election where issues in local politics were firmly bound together with national ones. The election saw the Conservative/ Unionist coalition of Balfour swept from power (collapsing from 402 seats to 157) by a tide in favour of the Liberals under Campbell-Bannerman. To contemporaries though, the talking point was not so much the decisive Liberal victory, for that had been expected, but the emergence of Labour as a real force in British politics. In addition to 24 Lib-Lab candidates, the parliamentary Labour party gained 29 seats. This was the most significant outcome of the election to Balfour as it was to *The Times* newspaper.[21] The significance of the Liberal victory lay more in the future with a series of social reforms, all of which were to have an impact on the provision of care, particularly for the elderly. Within two years of their victory, the Old Age Pensions Act of 1908 gave five shillings a week to every person over the age of 70 provided they passed a means test. The nature of this change was to introduce some concept of state provision by entitlement as opposed to seeking relief either through the Poor Law system or through charity. To the Bristol Municipal Charities, increasing state provision forced them to rethink their role as welfare providers, not only from the point of view of having to judge where best to allocate resources, but also because they came in for particular censure from interest groups determined to see the influence of endowed charity diminish and their funds redistributed.

20 *op. cit.,* p. 17
21 Asa Briggs, *The Political Scene,* in Simon Nowell-Smith, ed., *Edwardian England 1901-1914,* 1964, pp. 52-53

CHAPTER 2
Charity

The Concept of Charity

Studying charity in an historic, urban context can be looked at from two contrasting viewpoints; the extent to which it either imposed order on its recipients or that it represented social consensus. The first debate rests on the notion that charity was provided by wealthy elites who used it as a device to control society; by handing out money and help in kind, they attempted to create dependence amongst the poor. The second argument reflects the huge number of people in all ranks of society who were involved in charitable work, and that its provision could be initiated by ordinary citizens. To some degree, the difference depends on which historical period is being analysed as the latter argument reflects the expansion of charitable giving during the Victorian period.[1] This was also a time when arguments ensued as to the benefits that charity provided. If we take the turn of this century as a benchmark, many liberal critics of philanthropy saw provision of charity as having negative effects on its recipients, alleging it posed a threat to individual liberty and responsibility. Most commentators, however, including the future instigator of the welfare state, William Beveridge, were enthusiastic about its contribution alongside state support.[2]

Charity is the voluntary giving of help through private or corporate action. It usually seeks to define the recipient to whom aid is being given, and to make sure that only genuine cases which meet the criteria laid down by the charity receive assistance. Specifically, the Bristol Municipal Charities was an endowed charity, and so functioned within a legal framework where money, land and buildings were left in a series of wills. The annual income from investments, sales and rent were then used to support a scheme, the details of which were specified by the donor. Trustees provided guidance on policy, and contributed to an administration which ensured continuity of purpose. Indeed, it was in this 'self perpetuating nature' that the strength of endowed charity lay.[3] By 1906, the BMC was an elite, endowed charity surviving in a sea of voluntarism and local government provision.

The BMC was created in 1836 by the Municipal Corporations Act, after reform of local government in Bristol. Before the mid 1830s, the city witnessed an intense struggle against corruption in local goverment, with the Bristol Riots of 1831 being the most explosive outbreak of popular protest against the Corporation. One of the outcomes of reform was that individual charities which were under Corporation control — and it must be remembered that most of the individual endowments had their origins in the sixteenth and seventeenth centuries when the only civic body that could provide trustees was the Corporation — were amalgamated and passed to a new, independent body, henceforth called the Bristol Municipal Charities (although quite a few of the old faces from the previous regime were appointed as trustees). All records, capital and interest of the endowments were transferred to the new charity trustees. The principal reason for this transfer was on account of the incontestable accusation that the City Corporation had misappropriated finances from charity accounts into its

1 See introduction to Martin Gorsky, *Charity, mutuality and philanthropy, 1800-70*, Unpublished Ph.D. thesis, A4409, University of Bristol, 1995

2 F. K. Prochaska, *Philanthropy* in F.M.L. Thompson ed., *The Cambridge Social History of Britain 1750-1850*; vol. 3, *Social Agencies and Institutions*, 1990, p. 392

3 Gorsky, *op. cit.*, p. 70

own coffers. One estimate put the misappropriation at £344,000 which was almost equivalent to the value of the estate in 1835. The Corporation's plan books, showing details of its property holdings before reform, show the Charities' properties well and truly combined into one portfolio instead of being administered separately. Wrangling over these and other issues went on for years with some concessions from the Corporation who passed over moderate sums in compensation. But generally, the 'reformed' Council's argument was that it was not liable for the sins of its predecessor.[4]

The BMC continued to act as a managing agent, collecting and distributing finances on behalf of the various individual, endowed charities that formed the sum of its parts.[5] These included three charity schools: the Free Grammar, The Red Maids and Queen Elizabeth's Hospital. In addition, there were 57 non-educational charities, consisting mainly of gifts and shelter which included: loan money; money and gifts to parish poor; provision of sermons; setting the poor to work; aid to poor prisoners; help to poor tradesmen; gifts to the blind; aid to almshouse poor; aid for poor lying-in-women (childbirth) and alms-houses — Foster's, Trinity and Bengough's.[6] Although the Municipal Charities worked corporately, its function was still to look after the individual interests of the charities that made up its whole by following the wishes of the respective donor. So, for example, the name of an individual charity is always assigned against property or share transactions and incomes. Exchanges of property from one charity to another within the organisation followed the same procedures the BMC conducted with external organisations. Undertaking the role of co-ordinating smaller units cut down on administrative costs and increased the efficiency and performance of the endowments.

In terms of expenditure, the majority of funding was devoted to educational provision and helping the aged through almshouse care or eleemosynary (charitable handouts) distribution although, and this is a later feature of their work, they provided some assistance to help the impoverished to emigrate as an extension of their remit in setting the poor to work.[7] In 1906, its 21 trustees managed and distributed annually about £30,000, making it the wealthiest of the endowed charities in Bristol. The number of annuitants, pensioners and annual grantees totalled about 400 and included 146 alms-people and 81 almshouse pensioners; about 600 people received gifts and donations.[8] The provision of charity by non-conformist churches and parishes, too, cannot be underestimated, as the latter were responsible for the majority of endowments. There were also other, long established charities which had never come into the Corporation fold of which Colston's Almshouses and Colston's School are well-known examples.

Endowment as a means of provision, however, was not the most popular form of charity by the time these photographs were taken. The nineteenth century had witnessed a huge expansion in sub-scription societies and mutual associations, the two principal forms of charitable institution which constituted voluntarism. In the late Victorian period, voluntarism, principally through donations of money, was well practised both amongst the working as well as the middle classes and, in the 1890s, the latter spent more of their budget on charity than any other single item of expenditure, with the exception of food.[9]

In 1906 Bristol was awash with voluntary charities. Health provision and attention to the welfare of children formed perhaps the two most prominent areas of benevolence, but in truth, the choice

---

4 For an overview of the change of administration, see Graham Bush, *Bristol And Its Municipal Government 1820-1851*, Bristol Record Society, vol. xxix, 1976, pp. 155-156. The collation of working practices to make the Charities function as a unit was not fully complete until the 1890s.

5 See appendix 1 for full list

6 Bush, *op. cit.,* p. 67

7 See in general BMC *Emigration Book,* c.1912

8 J. W. Arrowsmith, *Dictionary of Bristol 1906*, pp. 61-66

9 Prochaska, *op. cit.*, p. 358

was extensive and the city had the highest range of provision outside London, leading the BMC's Secretary to write that 'There is probably no city in the Kingdom, which in proportion to its population, is more abundant in charities than is the city of Bristol'.[10]

As examples, potential benefactors in Bristol could choose from institutions still familiar to us such as Muller's Orphanage at Ashley Down, which catered for up to 2050 children, and the National Incorporated Waifs' Association, Ever Open Door (better known as Barnardo's Homes). Less familiar organisations and institutions included: the House of Rest for Women by the Downs opened by Queen Victoria in 1897; The Guild of the Poor Things for helping the blind, crippled and maimed; the Gloucestershire Society, Grateful Society and the Dorcas Society, all of which assisted poor, married women in childbirth; the Preventive Mission which rescued young girls from 'perilous associations' and prepared them for domestic service; Devonians in Bristol who promoted 'friendly intercourse between Devonians resident in Bristol, and all measures tending to increase the prosperity of the County of Devon'; the Emigration Society to advise would-be emigrants, and the Bristol Blanket Lending Society whose purpose was to lend blankets from November to June; there were five grades of blanket, the newest and warmest of which were reserved for those who had an exemplary record of caring for previously lent coverings.[11] Then there was the Children's Country Visiting Society which 'sent sick children under the age of 12 into the fresh air and the homes of kindly people for one to three weeks vacation'; about 500 children annually received help. The Children's Help Society, which was founded in 1884, concentrated its efforts during winter time in the inner city, providing cheap dinners and nearly 100,000 free breakfasts annually and in summer, sent hundreds of children to a camp near Winscombe in Somerset.[12]

Perhaps the best example of a mutual association at this time was the Guild of Help Movement which began in Bradford in 1905, and was soon established in Bristol. Its aim was to impart a civic character to charitable work and to bring citizens of all classes together. It co-operated with the Poor Law, Public Health and Education Boards in order to effect its programme.[13]

The survival of endowed charities was becoming less usual by the end of the nineteenth century. Indeed, philanthropy as a whole was making less contribution to the relief of poverty by this time. In the BMC's case, and we are talking here of its urban element, one has to remember that the majority of its constituent charities were formed in the sixteenth and seventeenth centuries when the population of Bristol was around 10-12,000 people. In 1906 even the declining inner city could muster four times this population, so the Municipal Charities barely touched the surface of need by twentieth century standards. That is not to diminish the contribution of endowed or voluntary charity, however. The annual pattern of Poor Law relief in Bristol follows that of the country as a whole for the late Victorian and Edwardian periods, albeit that the number of people receiving relief in the city is consistently less than the national average.[14] One explanation for this could be the generally more favourable economic conditions in the Bristol area, with its very diverse industrial base leading to less unemployment problems, but recessions did hit the city from time to time so this could not account for the stable gap between the national average and the Poor Law Union's expenditure. It is tempting to point to Bristol's capacities in the range and amount of charitable benevolence as being an important constant that filled the gap. Some idea of the relative importance of charity can be seen from returns to the House of Commons in 1893, which estimated the annual revenue from endowments in the city as

10 Frederick Newton, Secretary to the Bristol Charity Trustees quoted in *Bristol As It Was* etc., p. 256
11 Arrowsmith, *op.cit.*, p. 72
12 *Wright's Bristol Directory 1906*
13 See in general C.L. Mowat, *The Charity Organisation Society 1869-1913, Its Ideas and Works*, 1961
14 See Archer et al., *Abstract of Bristol Historical Statistics. Part 1. Poor Law Statistics 1835-1948*, University of the West of England, 1997, *Table 6* and p. xvii.

£58,126,[15] whilst the expenditure on outdoor and indoor relief for the Bristol Union in September 1893 was £9,312.[16]

This raises an issue as to the extent to which charities were in competition with state organisations or supplemented them, and, therefore, lowered the cost of Poor Law relief for the ratepayer. On the one hand the Municipal Charities provided 'indoor relief' in its care for the elderly, as did the workhouse, and in its other benevolent capacity provided 'outdoor relief' by way of pensions and annuities. The extent to which these capacities overlapped or that there was either conflict or co-operation between providers was of concern to late Victorian social enquirers as is apparent from the enquiry into the Bristol poor in 1884 [17] and a Royal Commission into provision for the aged poor in 1895.[18] One group, the Bristol Charity Organisation Society, endeavoured to bring into co-operation with each other, and with the Poor Law authorities, the various charitable agencies and individuals in the city. In effect, it set itself up as a non-statutory regulator which aimed to prevent waste and check imposture. In this sense, it followed the concerns of the author of the report into *The Condition of the Bristol Poor* in seeking to prevent duplication of effort or double applications for benefit. The Charity Organisation Society had no funds of its own, but acted as an agent to send what they deemed worthy applicants in the direction of other agencies. In 1908, the Civic League of Personal Service was formed. It enlisted the assistance of citizens as 'visitors', each one undertaking the care and oversight of two or three families. They did not give relief in money or kind either, but brought needy cases before the League committee. The aim was to prevent charity finding its way to undeserving cases.[19] The regulating body to which the Municipal Charities had to accede was the Charity Commissioners in London, an organisation founded in 1853 with the purpose of collecting information about charitable trusts and acting as a national regulator of registered charities. Basically, the BMC had to inform the Charity Commissioners of certain actions they undertook, from supplying copies of expenditure and income, as well as seeking permission prior to undertaking major transactions such as buying, selling or exchanging assets.[20] From 1899, following the Education Act of that year, they also had to inform the Board of Education in London of financial arrangements with respect to education charity funds (although the jurisdiction over the properties remained with the BMC) and changes within the curriculum.[21]

15 *Bristol As It Was* etc., p. 256

16 See Archer et al., *Table 6:* the comparison needs to bear in mind that the boundaries for these two analyses do not coincide exactly.

17 *Report Of The Committee To Inquire Into The Condition Of The Bristol Poor, 1884*, edited by the Reverend S. A. Walrond, Vicar of St Lawrence Jewry in London. The report was originally commissioned under the auspices of the Bishop of Bristol.

18 *Royal Commission on the Aged Poor*, 1895. The report is analysed in chapter 5

19 *Bristol As It Was* etc., p.256

20 Hence, we can find out aspects of the BMC's *modus operandi* through correspondence between them and the Charity Commissioners, as well as an external analysis of the Municipal Charities' effectiveness in the Commissioners' Reports.

21 See, for example, letter of 15 November 1905 with respect to the Bristol Grammar School amongst similar correspondence in Letter Book F (*BMC Commissioners' Letter Book* 1903-07)

CHAPTER 3

The Properties

Managing

The Bristol Municipal Charities were first and foremost property holders. It was the income from this asset that allowed them to undertake their role as a charity. Their portfolio ran the gamut of urban stock; from domestic, industrial, warehousing and commercial sites, to renting out space for telephone lines and advertising on hoardings, although the bulk of its property was let to business uses; the individual captions to the photographs emphasise the immense variety of trades and commercial organisations that were in Bristol at the time. Since the Charities' property schedules reflect the composition of the inner city, they provide an easier source than trade directories for coming to initial conclusions about land use in the centre. What they exemplify is the sheer range of industrial and commercial use found. They indicate three principal development zones other than the banking and insurance concentration in the Broad Street and Corn Street area: a light manufacturing industrial zone that spread from Redcross Street to Broadweir, and the St Philip's area, both of which were based on water and rail transport routes; and a mixed light industrial and commercial zone around Redcliffe. In and amongst these businesses were to be found the homes of those who lived in the city.[1] As is the case today, each of these uses had its own market in terms of rental value and in ease of letting. Another issue for any property holder is consolidation; it is much more effective to manage a group of buildings adjacent to each other than the same number spread over a large area — so, where exactly was BMC property in Bristol and did their trustees attempt to consolidate holdings? This chapter outlines other issues, such as how they maintained and let out property, and whether letting had a charitable dimension in itself, i.e. were houses leased to disadvantaged groups? Also, how efficient were they at collecting rents and in achieving income? What were the external factors which impinged on their organisation and how were these dealt with?

The responsibility for the urban properties was undertaken by their appointed architects, Foster and Wood, and a surveyor. The former were long-standing consultants who undertook design and construction of new buildings and draughted architectural plans of the properties — the plan books they created give detailed arrangements of the floor plans of each property and their dimensions. The control of the stock was the responsibility of the surveyor of the urban properties, Frank Wills (of the tobacco family), assisted by a clerk-of-works. Wills had been appointed following a decision by the Trustees to advertise for a surveyor in April 1904. His duties were also to prepare plans of the city properties; survey and inspect all premises at least once every five years and, if practicable, on the falling in of a lease; conduct a revaluation every seven years (which is actually more of an estate agent's skill); see that leaseholders obeyed the terms of the lease; order and supervise work and personally oversee work over the value of £20 for which contract specifications had to be supplied, and report on property which the Trustees were considering purchasing.[2]

1 See appendix 2
2 BMC *Miscellaneous Minute Book*, p. 38

Subletting was allowed, although this was theoretically controlled, and tenants subletting without permission were refused renewal of their lease.[3] His letters advising the Trustees of actions to undertake with respect to their various property holdings, as well as the minutes of their committee meetings, are the two principal sources for trying to understand their approach to property management. These documents clearly emphasis a policy of consolidation wherever possible, both to enhance the value of holdings and to make management easier. The trustees were also anxious to attain property which blighted or impinged on existing holdings, either with the intention to demolish and rebuild or to improve. The two methods employed in order to achieve these strategies were purchase or exchange. Finances for purchase were accomplished through the sale of debentures and stock, whilst exchange was almost exclusively conducted with the Corporation of Bristol, the biggest individual landholder by far in the city. However, there are incidences of them approaching individual owners with the aim of persuading them to sell, receiving offers of property from individual or corporate owners and buying at auction. Arrangements for exchange with the Corporation were conducted on the basis of mutual rationalisation for both parties, or out of necessity when improvement schemes demanded the widening of a street and the demolition of, or alteration to, a Charities' property. The following case studies demonstrate the procedures and complexities of management which, if not the most exciting of issues, are important in emphasising the underlying, constant changing nature of property ownership which is not apparent from the photographs.

A good example of its dealings with the Council was an exchange of property between the Corporation of Bristol and the Trustees which gave the Trinity Hospital charity 'a house and shop at 48 Old Market Street with warehouse and lofts in the rear'.

This was a property 27 feet wide by 97 feet deep, a Medieval burgage plot in fact. In return Trinity handed over a strip of land on Unity street, most of which was on open ground. The surveyor recommended the exchange to the BMC Trustees on the basis that the land was of little use to the Charities and, indeed, might very well have to be given up to the Corporation under compulsory purchase powers. This deal also got them a strip of land on Unity Street adjacent to property belonging to Whitson's charity which, 'is of little use to the Corporation on account of its its being dominated by ancient lights ineligible for building on, but is of great importance to the Trustees, as it affords frontage to a greatly improving street for land and buildings extending 140 ft behind it into Jacob street, which is little more than a back lane, & very unlikely to improve'.[4] A third feature of the exchange to the benefit of the BMC was part of a hay and chaff warehouse on Host Street which extended the size of an adjacent property belonging to the Bristol Grammar School. To the Charities, it was always a question of anticipating the potential compulsory purchase price of property for street widening and weighing up the advantages and disadvantages of such an outcome.

In a letter to the Charity Commissioners in 1905, the BMC proposed an exchange of land between Whitson's Charity and the Corporation of Bristol which would give the Charities number 43 Old Market Street: 'This and two other houses, which the Trustees hope to secure hereafter when opportunity offers, will complete a fine block of property admirably situated for trade purposes in a main thoroughfare of considerable commercial importance and in close proximity to the St Philip's Station of the Midland Railway'.[5] The Council would acquire the Dutch House in exchange, which the BMC was keen to dispose of since it was in a dilapidated state and the potential repair bill too expensive to contem-

3 BMC *Committee Minutes,* 23 February 1906
4 Handwritten copy of report, 24 February 1891
5 Letter to Charity Commissioners, 23 February 1905
6 BMC *Charity Commissioners' Letter Book,* 20 February 1905

plate.[6] The Council's intention was then to demolish the building for street widening. Eventually, this famous feature of Bristol's pre-war landscape was only saved on the casting vote of the Lord Mayor in 1909. The deal between the Corporation and Charities was concluded in 1906 and also gave the BMC a section of vacant land in Pile Street under the control of the Health Committee, a ground rent issuing out of 50 Old Market Street, a property that was on the corner with Lawford Street and a ground rent secured on the Red Maids' School.[7] The property on Pile Street, Redcliffe had a frontage of 160 feet and an average depth of 110 feet. To the BMC, its acquisition had the benefit of consolidating ownership with existing property on Portwall Lane. 'By throwing the whole into one property I am positive the value thereof would be greatly increased' remarked the Trustees' Secretary.[8] The value of the Corporation's interest had been agreed at £4073 12s. 6d. and that of the Trustees at £3900, leaving a sum of £173 12s.6d. to be paid by the Charities. The time gap in coming to a successful conclusion in this case is worth noting because of the scale and value of the exchange which needed discussion in committee by both the Corporation and the Trustees. The time span was exacerbated by the Charity Commissioners, to whom the Secretary of the Trustees wrote expressing dismay that they had imposed a requirement that the Corporation pay the costs and expenses on the exchange. The Secretary was of the opinion that since both parties were gaining equally, both should pay, and further reminded the Commissioners that they had not imposed a restriction on a similar exchange of property in 1892:

I have been in communication with the Corporation Officials in regard to the proposed condition, and they urge that the costs should be shared, the transaction being as much in the interests of the Trustees as in those of the Corporation. There is no doubt that this is so especially as the acquisition of the house at No. 43 Old Market Street is so important to the Charity.[9]

Number 43 Old Market Street was a dwelling house and draper's shop at the intersection of Redcross Lane and Old Market Street. The buildings, although old, were 'in a fairly tenentable state — an expenditure of some £20 would probably be needed on the property which is now void. The present rent of the property is £40 per year; previously to the year 1901 it was let at £42 per year'.[10] Frank Wills, the surveyor, valued the property at £750. Several windows in the Redcross Lane frontage of number 43 dominated the northern block of Trinity Hospital. If the height of the building was raised in the future it would have a deleterious effect upon the lights of the almshouse; a successful purchase would prevent this problem. On account of these factors, both surveyor and Foster and Wood strongly recommended the acquisition of number 43, as this would further consolidate a block of seven properties that the Charities owned on the same side of Old Market Street, with the proposition that they buy number 42 if it came up for sale, as this druggist's shop, dwelling house and warehouse was the only remaining structure that stood in the way of a complete sequence of ownership.[11]

The Trustees relied on the advice of their architects and surveyor in making decisions concerning property amalgamation, repair and disaggregation. Following such advice, they gave sanction for improvement to 104 and 105 Temple Street, property belonging to Queen Elizabeth's Hospital, the total bill of which came to £968. The buildings were in 'a most disgraceful and uninhabitable condition which ...is only kept together by shoring with props' and had been condemned by the local authority as long ago

7 *Report of the Estates and General Purposes Committee*, 13 February 1906

8 BMC *Charity Commissioners' Letter Book*, 20 February 1905. In the following year, the land was developed with the Trustees contributing £3000, to the new tenant's £1000, on a 30 year lease; see BMC *Committee Minutes*, 23 February 1906

9 BMC *Charity Commissioners' Letter Book*, 18 March 1905

10 Letter from Foster and Wood, 27 July 1904

11 Letter by Foster and Wood to Frederick Newton, the Charities' Secretary, 22 February 1905

as 1888.[12] To raise the requisite finance they sold shares in Bristol Waterworks and other companies to the tune of £469, obtained £10 from 5% preference shares and charged the balance to a sinking fund which they opened specifically for QEH to make provision for expenditure.[13]

In a separate case, the Trustees had been endeavouring for some time to acquire three cottages, but without success, on account of the life tenant being unwilling to sell. But the property being offered for sale by auction, on the recommendation of Wills, they placed a bid for £360 on behalf of Whitson's, the aim being to acquire a block of properties adjacent to one already owned by this charity.[14] On occasions they were offered property for sale by individuals; they declined an offer of property on St Augustine's Parade, for example, around Easter 1906.[15]

On a previous occasion, the BMC sold properties at 54 and 55 Thomas Street, and four cottages on Mitchell Lane, to Weston Estates on the basis that the properties were partially sited in a side street away from the main thoroughfare, and 'partly in a narrow lane of squalid buildings and of little importance commercially'. The buildings were of the poorest type and almost in ruinous condition and there was concern that the proposed widening of Mitchell Lane by the Council would leave them with an awkward, wedge-shaped piece of land which would seriously impair its value for building purposes.[16] Weston promptly pulled them down and constructed a warehouse on site, a small but significant action which exemplifies one way in which Tudor and Stuart houses in this area were replaced by Victorian and Edwardian commercial buildings. In turn, these warehouses have largely gone, initially victims of the blitz, and then post-war planning which designated the area an industrial development zone.

Turning to the question as to whether or not the BMC was considerate in finding solutions to the housing problems that Bristol faced in the innner city, a report from Wills to the weekly committee confirms the hardnosed approach they took to managing their assets. When referring to Ash Lodge cottages, which belonged to Temple and Whitson charities, he remarked that it is 'doubtful whether it would not pay the Trustees to keep these cottages void, they being of such a character as are only suitable for a very poor class of tenants who are generally migratory in their habits, and constant changing of tenants involves considerable expense, which often I believe counterbalances the rent'.[17]

Caring for property

The Bristol Municipal Charities invariably agreed to tenants' suggested changes to the structure of property which added to its value, as long as the work was monitored by their surveyor and did not impinge on their finances; for example, they gave permission for a loft to be added at 107 Redcliffe Street, but declined to contribute to the tenant's costs.[18] They also allowed George Vosper Paget, a tenant at 9 Peter Street, to provide a new staircase and an enlargement to the kitchen at his own expense.[19] They were prudent managers of properties, too; there were only five defaulters listed in their *Arrears of Rent* book, one of whom was already under notice,[20] and their *Property Repair Reports* are a testimony to the care expended on buildings.

An example was the work required in the reinstatement of dilapidation on 50 Old Market Street, held on a lease by the Swift Beef Company, which

12 Reference to letter of surveyor to the BMC Board of Trustees, *BMC Committee Minutes*, 2 February 1906

13 BMC *Committee Minute Book 15*, p. 614

14 BMC *Charity Commissioners' Letter Book*, 20 January 1905

15 BMC *Committee Minutes*, 23 March 1906

16 BMC *Charity Commissioners' Letter Book*, 2 June 1904

17 See also BMC *Finance Committee Minutes*, 23 March 1906. These are Ash Cottages (Ash Lodge) in Temple which had been purchased at auction in 1902 for £24 7s. in order to complete the ownership of a complex of buildings used as warehousing (see photograph nos. 11-13). One of the surviving plans shows that the cottages were demolished at some point and a store built on the site (Plan Book no 101)

18 BMC *Committee Minutes*, 23 February 1906

19 BMC *Committee Minutes*, 10 March 1906

20 BMC *Arrears of Rent Book*, 1902 onwards

expired on 29 September 1906. This lease covered a series of buildings over which there had been protracted discussions between the Charities and the meat company with respect to the cost of renewal. From an original demand of £90 which was declined by the company, the surveyor advised the Trustees to renew at a reduced rental of £80 as being preferable to having the property void.[21] In this case the Swift Beef Company were existing tenants, but the predominate means by which the Charities found new tenants was to advertise in the local papers, although occasionally, they resorted to public auctions as a method.[22]

Refurbishments at 50 Old Market Street included: repainting the window frames in the attic with three coats and repairing the window board; cutting out and renewing broken plastering on the second floor staircase; fixing a new 1/- fastener to the window in the front room on the second floor; providing new sash cords to windows on the first floor and connecting the privies to the Bristol Waterworks Company's supply.[23] Quite what the situation was with regard to water supply to the Charities' residential properties in the early twentieth century is not clear, but in 1896 the number of such properties without direct water supply to clear away sewerage was extensive. The vast majority of such houses, 84 in total, lacked a direct water supply to the privy. The Charities deemed that about half of these properties would benefit from expenditure to lay on water. Reasons included the fact that the toilets opened directly into the respective houses, that houses were sub-let to lodgers or that they opened into confined courts. Where the houses were in open courts or had gardens, and were not inhabited by many people was justification to preclude invest-

ment.[24] It was not just the typical court cottage that lacked a direct supply. Of their Orchard Street properties, fine examples of Georgian architecture, and which were in good condition, nine lacked a a mains water connection.

Their precision in calculating costs, which is a reflection of careful management by their professional surveyor, on paint, fastenings and other items of expenditure can also be seen in the work completed on Red Maids' School in July 1906. The tower bedroom and box room was painted in *Duresco* and the walls repapered with 9d. paper. The entrance hall to the ground floor was redone in 1s. paper whilst the teachers' dining room got 2s. 6d. wallpaper and the matron's bedroom 2s. covering: truly, a hierarchy of costs.[25] Although work above £20 went out to tender, they relied on a core of tradesmen to make the maintenance as efficient as possible.[26]

In conclusion then, we have a charity careful in the administration of its property portfolio. Never generous with unnecessary expenditure, it took a business rather than a philanthropic attitude to spending money on improvements. Despite the undoubted fact that some of its properties were in poor condition, the surviving number of repair documents hint at a steady refurbishment programme.[27] When they did spend money on refurbishment, it was with the intention of capitalising through improved rental value. Property reserved for its own use — schools and almshouses — seems to have received priority when it came to expenditure. Above all, they were acutely aware of the economic dynamics of the urban property market, realising what factors improved financial return, knowing when to demolish rather than rebuild and having a long-term, strategic view to estate management.

21 *BMC Committee Minutes*, 9 March 1906

22 See, for example, the building site on Midland Road, photo no.47 and BMC *Committee Minutes*, 26 January 1906

23 *Repair Folder*, September 1906

24 *List of houses not supplied with water*, 25 March 1896

25 *Repair Folder*, July 1906

26 See BMC *Annual Report*, 1907

27 Looking at the condition of the exteriors in the photographic archive is the only method by which we can come to a conclusion on this point. Of course, this is all relative. Surviving photographs of slum housing in the Frogmore Street area in 1929 indicate the quite appalling state of some domestic property.

CHAPTER 4

Children

One aspect of life the photographic archive highlights is the clusters of children that frequented the streets of Bristol in the Edwardian period. The street life of the city, though not busy, is nevertheless extensively represented. The photographer did not intend to take pictures of people. His brief was the buildings, but inevitably people were captured on film in the process. So, we see children playing, hanging around on corners, possibly working in company with adults or looking after younger siblings. Documentary and oral history sources hint at all of these issues during this period and give a wide ranging analysis of the culture of the street from the perspective of both the authorities and of children themselves. None of these children are in school, further proof that some of the photographs are likely to have been taken in the morning or at a weekend (a significant number of the photographs show boys dressed in their best clothes and wearing Eton collars); alternatively, they might suggest that there was some truancy from school.

By 1906, education was compulsory until at least the age of 12.[1] Whilst supply met demand with respect to primary education, the potential applicants for secondary school education exceeded the number of free places available, and so it was a system, like that of the grammar schools, which was dominated by the middle classes or the skilled working-class.[2] Working-class families who still remained in the 'old city' probably lacked a sense of interest in educating their children. This disinterest was both cultural, as well as hidebound by necessity, and the charity schools failed them as much as the state system particularly on account of the number of potential candidates living within a stone's throw of two of the BMC's schools — Queen Elizabeth's Hospital and Red Maids.

State Schooling

State provision itself, i.e. payment for schooling being levied on the rates, had only come in with the Elementary Education Act (1870) although some contribution by parents was demanded with even the poorest being required to pay a penny a week initially. Elementary education was administered under the School Board system which started in Bristol in 1871, but was reformed in 1903 when the various committees that made up the Board were amalgamated into the Bristol Education Committee. The Education Act (1880) finally made schooling compulsory for all children, and when education provided free at the point of delivery became available, this removed the financial barriers for pupils to access a basic education. Up to that point, the role of providing free education had been filled by two of the three schools under BMC management, so one question which needs to be addressed is the extent to which their establishments continued a need to educate the poor now that free state education was provided, and why parents wanted to send their children to charity schools.

Although one respondent to the Report on the Bristol Poor made the comment that 'Many think that there is no better way of spending charity money than in education', with the availability of state education a more widespread view existed that

---

1 Provided a child had reached Standard VII in the elementary system. The leaving age was up to 14 years of age for those who did not.
2 Stephen Humphries, *Hooligans or Rebels? An Oral History of Working-Class Childhood and Youth 1889-1939*, p. 53

there was no better use for charitable endowments 'than to apply them towards the extinction of the national debt' or to assist emigration.[3]

The new, local authority school system experienced subversion from pupils both in terms of classroom indiscipline and truanting, although overall the Bristol School Board (Education Committee from 1903) achieved a good success rate in keeping their charges within school premises. The average attendance for the city hinged around the 88% mark in the first decade of the new century but this does not reflect the blips of quite severe non-attendance which could send it dipping down to 80%, as it did at Christmas 1904 when there was an outbreak of diphtheria, and parents kept their children at home for fear of them catching it.[4] The attendance figure for the accounting year ending March 1906 gives an annual average of 89% but this provides a cautionary tale in the analysis of such statistics as it is clear that there was confusion which resulted in the non-accounting, for registration purposes, of scholars absent through illness; the real absence figure was obviously higher.[5] 'Mooching', a Bristol term for truanting, partly explains non-attendance. This was only one headache with which the authorities had to contend, but as the following testimony demonstrates, they could be tough on offenders:

> ...we'd get murdered if we mooched ...God you'd get half murdered if you done that. Although a lot of the boys used to do it, and they used to get put away, they used to get put away in a reformatory school. And where our school was, Clifton National, the reformatory school was like down there and we were up here. And in our school our desks was up on platforms and we used to be able to look down and look into the reformatory yard where the boys used to have to do their drills and that, and their band practice.[6]

Despite the fact that these boys reasons for absconding represent no more than a general frustration and boredom with school life, the effects of poverty or necessity as factors in causing truancy cannot be ignored. It is a feature well known in rural contexts because of the seasonal nature of work at harvest time particularly, but it occurred in cities as well. Bunking off school to help parents with work in times of necessity and having to look after siblings whilst a mother went out to work were two reasons why pupils might be absent from school. There were also endemic diseases like scarlet fever and measles, and 'alternative curricula' organised for the pupils by other organisations. Some of the best material for giving an insight into these problems lie in the numerous school log-books that survive.[7] 'Attendance poor, owing to Sunday School outings' lamented the headteacher of Sussex Street School (29 June 1906). He also faced constant lateness or non-attendance from children who lived in the Blackfriars district of his catchment area. The first day of term could result in a poor show as Castle Park Junior School found: 'Re-opened school. Attendance very poor, 100 children' (9 September 1905). The same comments permeate the log books of other schools. Attendance very poor this morning' and 'Attendance this afternoon very low, only fiftynine [sic] present' (Mina Road 18 July and 29 June 1901). Other schools faced slightly more difficult problems. Park Row Industrial School for Boys, one of the very establishments to which the truants, referred to by Nellie Bowl (in the quotation above), were sent, took the boys to the Downs one September afternoon. 'F. Strivens absconded' wrote the head in his log book; two days later the lad was picked up at Swindon (13 September 1906). The local authority employed attendance officers to catch miscreants — 'I have drawn the attendance officers' notice to some children who habitually absent themselves once or twice weekly' noted the head of St Augustine's Girls

---

3 *Report Of The Committee To Inquire Into The Condition Of The Bristol Poor,* 1884, p.132
4 Bristol Education Committee, *Annual Report 1905,* p.53
5 Bristol Education Committee, *Annual Report 1906,* p.23
6 *Bristol People's Oral History Project,* recording no.11: p.24 of transcript: Nellie Bowl, born Hotwells 1897
7 The following references are all to school log books, classified under School Records in the Bristol Record Office

School in her log book (1 February 1907). Unfortunately, the usual terse one-liners in the log books do little to make us realise the reasons for personal decisions made by children and parents who avoided attendance. An earlier series of records from the boys' school at St Augustine's provides a number of interesting case studies written up at length by the headteacher which help to flesh out what was still a common problem in the early twentieth century, of which this is one example:

Alexander Armstrong has been absent since Monday. I have several times asked his brother where he is and he today has told me that he has gone to Newport with his father for a short time and will come to school when he returns. Scarcely believing this I have enquired of the other boys in the school and find that about a score of them have seen Alexander about the streets today and other days helping another with a donkey and cart to sell coals. (19 February 1885)

But there were genuine reasons, too, as when five children had been absent from the girls school at St Augustine's for a significant period owing to an outbreak of scarlet fever (18 February 1907). To try and prevent such problems, the local authority tried to educate mothers about health matters at this time in order to get them to 'promote attention to health, cleanliness and comfort in the homes of our school-children throughout the city'.[8]

On the Streets

The street culture that resulted from these absences was only part of the overall scene. Without open space in which to play, children and youths found their own amusement, much of it very territorial, their world being confined to the streets that constituted their neighbourhood.[9] The lack of space to play within the inner city led the Education Com-

mittee to pass a resolution in 1906 'that having regard to the lack of public playgrounds in the older parts of the City, and the nuisance and danger to health and limb caused by children playing in the streets, the Elementary Education Committee be requested to consider and report upon the advisability of opening a few school playgrounds on Saturdays as an experiment.'[10] The playground scheme came into operation in September 1906 with voluntary charity support from the Children's Help Society and the Clarion Cinderella Society.[11]

Without such provision, the walls of buildings formed the backdrop to many street games (look at the chalk marks on the walls, presumably part of a ball game, that appear in photograph no. 62, for example) whilst the streets themselves became a playground:

Pitch and Toss was another game we used to play, in my day there was a blacksmith round the corner, we had steel hoops made, used to get some wire and weld it up, beat it up on the blacksmith's anvil and put a handle on it with a ring you know so the hoop was on the ring and then you could run down the road and keep this hoop going; it used to sing — zinnng — it would go along the cobbles, make a terrific noise, used to get people shouting at us when we were going past, ' Take those things away from here!' But this is the games we used to play.[12]

Larking about for working-class children formed part of street culture. Street pranks included stinging adults' bottoms with nettles through the rear flap doors of the outside lavatories; filling sugar bags with horse dung to tempt passers by to pick them up (and you will see from the photos that most of the streets are full of the stuff) or a game called 'ginger knocking' where children, removed at a safe distance from discovery, played havoc with their neighbours' peace.

8 Bristol Education Committee, *Annual Report 1906*, p. 29
9 See, in general, Stephen Humphries' works cited in Bibliography
10 Bristol Education *Committee Minutes*, 31 September 1906
11 Bristol Education Committee, *Annual Report 1907*
12 *Bristol People's Oral History Project*, recording no.64: p 58 of transcript

… we used to fix a safety pin in the door or in the glass of their windows on the side of their frame and you could get a bit of cotton and thread it through. Some houses had little frames around their windows, you could thread it over and get it up into about four doors up and hide in the passage up there and you would pull the cotton and the pin would clank against the window and they would come out and see who it was tapping at the window but they couldn't see the pin and that …we used to run them ragged when we were kids.[13]

Larking about often verged on the criminal. Street theft from stalls was not uncommon, a necessity in times of need to supplement what were often inadequate diets. One other crime, which we must remember dates from before the First World War, is reminiscent of the very modern problem of joy riding, but with perhaps a moral conclusion:

One fellow, he got caught for theft, stealing a car, 'cause there weren't many about and this car 'e stole was the vicar of St Mary, Redcliffe church and 'e returned the car back again. It was just and 'e put down on the car 'ow much 'e'd spent on petrol.[14]

Charity Education
The administration of each school within the Bristol Municipal Charities was under separate trusteeship (although the majority of governors were BMC appointees) which dealt with financial, curriculum and appointment processes, leaving the Bristol Municipal Charities with the job of managing the assets.

The Queen Elizabeth's Hospital
Popularly known as 'the City School' in 1906, Queen Elizabeth's Hospital was founded by John Carr, a Bristol soapmaker, who in his will in 1586 included provision:

to erect and found by due form of law in the City of Bristol in some convenient house which the Mayor and Aldermen shall appoint and prepare which I trust they will provide for conveniently An Hospital for bringing up of poor children, such as shall be born in the City of Bristol or in any part of the manor, lands, or tenements in Congresbury, and whose parents are deceased or dead or fallen into decay and not able to relieve them…[15]

This boy's school, modelled on Christchurch in London, was originally on the land of the Gaunt's estate, part of which was developed and laid out as Orchard Street from 1717 onwards. The number of boys educated was added to over time as the foundation continued to increase its endowments as in 1599, for example, when Richard Cole gave a yearly sum of £1 arising out of a house in Marsh Street, a tenement in Baldwin Street and land in the parish of St James.[16] Edward Colston added six boys in 1695 and a further four in 1702 to make a total of 44.[17] The endowments continued to accrue throughout the following centuries; in 1808 Samuel Gist left £10,000 on trust to provide for six poor men and six poor women and to maintain, educate and clothe six poor boys in Queen Elizabeth's Hospital and six poor girls for ever.[18] The present school on Brandon Hill opened in September 1847. The old school was used to provide better living conditions for local people. In 1865 the BMC leased the property to the Metropolitan Association for Improving the Dwellings of the Industrial Class, who rebuilt part of the west range to create a model dwelling which has the distinction of probably being the earliest block of flats in Bristol.[19]

13 *ibid.*
14 *Hooligans or Rebels?*, quoting Fred Harris, a member of a Bristol Street gang, p. 185
15 Walter A. Sampson, *History of Queen Elizabeth's Hospital*, p.13
16 Sampson, *op. cit.*, p.20
17 F.W.E. Bowen, *Queen Elizabeth's Hospital Bristol: the City School*, p. 32
18 C.M. MacInnes and W.F. Whittard eds., *Bristol and its Adjoining Counties*, p. 299
19 Keith Mallory, *The Bristol House*, 1985, p. 50

In 1875, the rules concerning Queen Elizabeth Hospital's foundation were changed slightly following a review of endowed charity schools by Parliamentary Commissioners, but its intake still continued to include 60 boys who were poor orphans having lost one or both parents, or children whose parents were incapacitated. Boys had to have been born in Bristol or have lived at least three years in the parliamentary borough. There was also an intake whose applicants must have attended a local authority school in Bristol for at least a year or have come from Congresbury. The subjects of instruction basically followed that of the state elementary and secondary school systems as the school taught boys from the ages of 8 to either 15 or 16.[20] The governors provided finance for scholarships as well as some aid for boys to emigrate.

The objective of the school by the turn of the century, therefore, was to provide education and maintenance for 160 foundation boarders, of whom 60 were orphans between 8 and 10 years of age on admission, and 100 elementary school boys between 10 and 12 years of age on admission. The actual number was less than this as the foundation boarders declined from 152 in 1885 to 127 by 1906 owing to a fall in income from rural property, a result of continued agricultural depression. The school made up the difference by increasing the fees paid by non-orphans and charging the elementary intake for uniforms.[21]

An analysis of the occupation of parents whose children attended QEH at this time shows how they mirrored the range of lower middle-class and semi- or skilled working-class occupations that were widespread in the city. They included: 7 school-masters and clerks; 19 small retailers and shop-keepers; 44 mechanics; 14 policemen and railway workers and officials; 16 factory workers and shop assistants; 5 lodging house keepers; 17 dressmakers and seamstresses; 12 domestic servants and char-women; 15 labourers and 10 pensioners with no occupation.[22]

The Red Maids' School

The Red Maids' School was founded in 1627 by Alderman John Whitson, a man who was well ahead of his time in setting up a specific remit to provide education for girls only. The original pupils were the daughters of dead or distressed burgesses. They were taught English, learnt to sew and to do other work to contribute to their maintenance. In 1906, the school was on Denmark Street, an establishment that had been built in 1840, and which was to be badly damaged in a fire in the October after the photographs were taken. The curriculum then was similar to a higher grade elementary school.[23] About £100 was granted annually for students to pursue studies in higher education, which normally meant teaching.

The school in 1906 contained 80 boarders, 50 places of which were reserved for girls who had lost one or both parents. Like QEH, there were two classes of entrant:

Class A — girls who are orphans, or who have lost one or both parents, or girls whose parents from mental or physical incapacity are unable to maintain them, such girls having been born or resident for three years within the boundaries for the time being of the Parliamentary Borough of Bristol, and to be eligible for admission between the ages of 8 and 10 years.

Class B — girls who have attended for at least one year a Public Elementary School within the boundaries of Bristol, such girls having been born or resident for three years within the

20 Bowen, *op. cit.,* p.111 and J.W. Arrowsmith, *Dictionary of Bristol*, 1906, p. 171. The curriculum for Standards 1 to VII in Elementary schools comprised English, Handwriting, Arithmetic, Drawing, Observation Lessons and Nature Study, Geography, History, Music and Physical Exercise, including Swimming for children aged 10 and upwards (Bristol Education Committee *Annual Report 1906* p. 38). Higher Grade Elementary schools provided manual training to boys over 12 years of age and girls had the additional subjects of Needlework and Domestic Economy which focused on cooking and laundry work.

21 Sampson, *op. cit.,* p. 89

22 Bowen, *op. cit.,* p. 114

23 i.e. an elementary system with the additional subjects of domestic economy, health and needlework; see footnote 20

boundaries, and to be eligible for admission between the ages of 10 and 12 years.[24]

The intake into each of these two classes reflects the difference in the social status of the girls, a factor that equally well applies to the boys who entered Queen Elizabeth's Hospital. Of the cohort who entered in 1906 under category A, the designation against the dead or surviving parent comprised cleaners, tailoresses, dressmakers, bootmakers, housekeepers, charwomen, masons, a mangling woman, a small shop owner, a machine-worker, a nurse, a labourer, an office cleaner, one occupied in sewing, and a girl being looked after by her grandmother, another by her aunt and another dependant on her uncle. Girls applying under the second classification had a parent or guardians who included a compositor, a wife of a cycle maker, a factory hand, a warehouseman, an engineer, the widow of a sanitary inspector, the wife of a bricklayer, a sheet-iron worker, a storekeeper, a police constable, an assurance agent, a labourer's wife, a house decorator, an engine driver, a railway clerk, a capsule maker and a grocer. The labourer excepted, all the occupations in the second category could be classified as skilled working class or clerical, whilst the orphans came from predominately unskilled backgrounds. What both groups had in common was that their entrees came from the same catchment area which concentrated on the southern and eastern suburbs of the city. Only one in the entire admission for that year came from what could be regarded as the centre — Winifred Nellie Davis, an orphan who lived with her grandmother at 9 Park Place, itself a BMC property.[25]

Bristol Grammar School

The BMC's third educational establishment was run on different principles. Firstly, it was essentially a day school — boarders were provided for in private digs.

Its Tyndall's Park base was built in 1879 to the design of the BMC's architects, Foster and Wood. The school taught 400 boys and provided the archetypal grammar curriculum — Latin, Greek, French, German, mathematics, physics and chemistry. Pupils had the choice of classical, or commercial and scientific training. Of all the Charities' schools, the Grammar was the one with the most obvious fee-paying structure, although a minimum of 25 places were paid for with Peloquin scholarships (i.e. with money from a BMC charity) on the basis of an annual competition, and there were also city scholarships paid for by the Corporation.[26] This admission policy was reflected in the social status of applicants. A random analysis of the intake for 1905 to 1906, for example, shows that the entrants' fathers came from occupations such as bookselling, publishing, photography and schoolteaching, or were clerks in holy orders, managers, agents or gentlemen.[27] It is clear that the aim of the Bristol Grammar School was to offer boys the opportunity to enter professions or proceed to higher education.

No records survive for what happened to pupils from QEH or Red Maids, save for the scholars. A comparison of this limited data seems to suggest that their education provided a small step up the social ladder when they eventually left the Municipal Charities' schools, and that perhaps the female leavers fared better than the boys. Around the turn of the century, girl scholars from the Red Maids' school most often entered the teaching profession either at Fishponds Training College or as pupil teachers, which is some reflection on the 'new' jobs open to young women at the turn of the century. Others became clerks, drapers' assistants, nurses, occasionally domestic servants and a few went to work at Pullen's or Campbell's dye works.[28] Of the boys from QEH who had been scholars, most became clerks; a few became Peloquin scholars at the Grammar School.[29]

24 *Admission Register*, BRO/33041/BMC/6/25e
25 *ibid*.
26 Arrowsmith, *op. cit.*
27 *Applications Register*, BRO/33041/BMC/3/A/3c
28 *Register of Occupation of Former Scholars*, BRO/33041/BMC/6/31
29 *Register of Occupations of Former Scolars*, BRO/33041/BMC/4/27a

From such a small sample, it is unwise to make too firm an analysis of the success of the Red Maids and Queen Elizabeth's Hospital, the two schools which equate more with the intake of the elementary school state system. But putting together the facets that have been covered, it perhaps hints at what distinguished these charity schools from local authority establishments and made them attractive to parents. Firstly, there were the contacts charity schools (and these were places with three to four hundred years of tradition) had with employers which could more or less guarantee employment to school leavers. Class sizes were smaller and discipline more effective, too. The Charities advertised scholarships and orphan places extensively in the press around May and November of each year, but allowed applications for interim vacancies as well. An entry examination applied to all entrants as did a medical. Consequently, their intake was small, defined and selective, yet their education accounted for the majority of the BMC's spending; over £14,000 per annum to educate no more than 436 children out of a school population of 66,000. Whilst the Red Maids and Queen Elizabeth's Hospital catered for 110 orphans between them, Muller's Orphanage, a rambling series of buildings on Ashley Down, looked after 2000 children in 1906.

Homes for Children

The BMC's long tradition in caring for needy children was, as their admission figures hint, a drop in the ocean in relation to need. By the 1890s, the child-saving movement had been well and truly hijacked by local and national bodies who had become the agents of control over not only compulsory schooling, but had also immersed themselves in the provision of leisure facilities, principally through church-related activities such as the temperance Band of Hope movement. One strong theme in child saving literature was the 'national disgrace of a drunken and dissolute slum culture', not a notion that was necessarily felt by the children themselves as oral history accounts are quite clear about their awareness of parental support. However, the dislocation of families in a strange urban environment, and the ever prevalent threat of disease, could have dire consequences for children left abandoned by a single parent or left without either:

Well the mothers or near enough the parents was out to work. They was never home then with kids then, as today ... Though they worked, but they loved their children. The trouble was when the mother and father died and they were left as orphans.[30]

The memory of events like these left some quite terrible recollections of what it was like in orphanages. Ivy Petherick, together with her brother and sister, was removed from her home in Barnstaple and placed in Muller's Orphanage, which was a charitable foundation, after the premature death of their mother and father:

I went to the orphanage in 1910, November 1910, I'll always remember. It was on a Monday morning, and a lady took the three of us there, me, my brother and sister. We arrived at this huge building, number 3. There were two thousand children in the five big homes altogether, and my brother was taken from us and taken to number 4. My sister was supposed to go to number 5 because she was quite young, but she wouldn't leave me — they could not part us. They were very strict, but it was no good — she was such a strong-willed child — so in the end, for the time being, they gave in. We were numbered. I was 381 and she was 382. We were taken to a changing-room and all our nice clothes that we had on were taken from us, and we put on calico chemises and calico knickers and a flannel petticoat and long black stockings. I found out eventually that we knitted them... I

30 *Bristol People's Oral History Project*, recording no. 24: p. 7 of transcript

*remember one or two girls coming in. I expect
they were very nervous; they did wet the bed.
And the poor dears, they were humiliated. They
were just held up to ridicule. They would be put
right down the end in the other dormitory, on a
straw bed, and that was their punishment.
Really, it was inhuman.*[31]

Technically, the responsibility for bringing up
homeless children at this time rested with the
Guardians of the Poor. They established three types
of home — a receiving home, 'scattered homes' all
over Bristol and a number of cottage homes out at
Downend. Each home had a foster-mother in charge.
The first type was a holding operation, the aim being
to place children in a receiving home until their
needs were assessed. The idea behind this reform
was to keep children out of the workhouse, where
formerly they had been educated, and to separate
them both from adult inmates and from institutional
methods. About 400 children were looked after in
this way. Others were fostered out to families and a
number sent to Canada through the Bristol Emigration Society.[32]

31 Quoted in *Hooligans or Rebels?*, p. 209
32 George Frederick Stone, *Bristol As It Was — And As It Is. A Record of Fifty Years' Progress*, p. 253

CHAPTER 5

The Elderly

The Bristol Municipal Charities provided benev-olence almost exclusively to two sectors of the com-munity — children and the elderly. The resources put into education generally benefited the able, but not impoverished child, which, as we have seen from the previous chapter, brought accusations of wasted expenditure against the organisation. In respect to its care of the elderly, the Charities also came in for criticism in the late nineteenth century for directing their resources inappropriately. Although the range of endowments they provided actually demonstrate quite a diverse series of doles and annuities for the poor, contemporary critics perceived the main problem to be the fact that the majority of their income was devoted, comparatively speaking, to serving very few people; if the income was targeted better some of the more acute problems faced by the elderly poor could be solved. 'Speaking generally, the large eleemosynary charities of Bristol are a source of pauperism, and in great measure will continue to be unwisely employed until collectively administ-ered' summed up one socialist critic's stance.[1] Not all critics agreed with this analysis, however, and in summing up the evidence presented to them in 1895, the Royal Commission on the Aged Poor could still 'attach much importance to the extended application of endowed charities for almshouses and pensions for the deserving aged poor …'.[2]

Prior to the introduction of a pension by the state in 1908, there was no satisfactory definition of old age. Evidence from Poor Law Union documents sug-gests that, around the turn of the century, 60 years of age and over basically put an individual into this category. The minimum age requirement for obtain-ing doles and annuities from the Bristol Municipal Charities was 50 years or over and for almshouse places, either 50 or 60 years (50 years of age was the expected life span at birth of the unskilled working class in 1900).

The need to provide for the aged poor in the inner city had certainly become acute by 1900. Rising unemployment generally had put many men near the end of their working life out of work; this problem was exacerbated by influxes of people from rural areas seeking work in the city because of agri-cultural depression.[3] With the move of a younger, and by now better educated population out of the city to the new suburbs, what was left in the centre was an older and poorer population. When Charles Booth looked into the plight of the aged poor in the 1890s, more than half the registered paupers in the Bristol Union area were aged 65 or over (54%) whilst the percentage of elderly paupers in the Barton Regis Union (part of which included Clifton) was 21%.[4] The discrepancy in the proportions can partly be explained by the expansion of Bristol at this time, causing social disruption which left some elderly without the traditional ties of kinship as their offspring migrated to the new suburbs. To some degree this was counterbalanced by other factors. The vicar of St Mary Redcliffe, in 1895, remarked that he had very little aged poverty in his parish:

1 *Facts for Bristol: An Exhaustive Collection of Statistical and Other Facts Relating to the City; With Suggestions for Reform on Socialist Principles*, Fabian Tract, no. 18, 1891, p. 13
2 *Royal Commission on the Aged Poor*, Part 1, par. 188
3 See the *Report Of The Committee To Inquire Into The Condition Of The Bristol Poor*, for this phenomenon in 1880s
4 Moira Martin, *Managing the Poor: The Administration of Poor Relief in Bristol in the Nineteenth and Twentieth Centuries* in Madge Dresser and Philip Ollerenshaw, eds., *The Making of Modern Bristol*, 1996, p. 161

While the majority of our people in Redcliffe belong to the working classes, we have not very much destitute poor. Again, our people have many special advantages. We have no less than 34 places in our almshouses which belong by right to them, and from our connection with the Merchant Venturers and the city authorities we can generally get admission to the other almshouses. A fair number of our people have Bonville, Dolphin or Anchor annuities.[5]

But the problem was severe in the east of the city. A vicar from one of the parishes there wrote to Mary Clifford, one of the Guardians for Barton Regis, in which he remarked:

I have for many years been compelled to notice that many aged folk of good character have suffered greatly through poverty, some of whom have not been in parish relief, and others have barely existed on the relief granted them by guardians …but they have been content to remain half-starved than go into the work-house.[6]

He had written to Clifford, one of the first women Guardians, at the time she was presenting evidence to the Royal Commission on the Aged Poor in 1895. A large number of benefactions went to the 'ancient city', but since a large proportion of the poverty of the city extended very much beyond the city bounds, Clifford was of the opinion that it would be of much better advantage if benefactions were available over a wider geographical area.[7] By way of follow up, she argued to the Commission that it was very difficult for any elderly person to get a city pension (but that the chances of success improved with age), despite the efforts of other vicars who tried to achieve it for members of their flock as a more dignified solution

to entering the workhouse.[8] This feeling was still current in 1906. The prospective Conservative candidate for Bristol West noted in his election address: 'My sympathies are strongly enlisted in favour of a thorough reform of our Poor Laws, whereby the Aged and Deserving poor may be freed from want without being driven to the workhouse'.[9] It is not an insignificant statement, for being sympathetic to the plight of the poor was traditionally more of a Liberal strongpoint than a Conservative one. The word 'deserving' is significant, too. That was the definition used by most philanthropists, of whatever political persuasion, to define those who should and those who should not get help. Mary Clifford who received the support of male, Liberal ratepayers in succeeding to become a Guardian was adamant on this point in her testimony to the Royal Commission. Elderly who drank were not deserving. The first dozen cases in a survey by the Board of Guardians' annual report for 1907-08 identifies drunkenness as the principal reason why these elderly poor entered the Stapleton workhouse.[10]

What constituted a deserving case is impossible to define, but those who had been thrifty during their lifetime, and had run out of money through having to spend it on surviving in old age, is perhaps the most common re-occurring model; working class people took this definition as being gospel, too. Even the deserving were often excluded from charity help and had to rely on outdoor relief from the Guardians. Clifford included the likes of those who had saved for their own tombstones, but had subsequently fallen on hard times. Quite why they failed to find charitable help was a mystery to contemporaries as there were enough funds, potentially, to match need to those who *deserved* it (although this ignored the huge demand that was out there from the elderly population as a whole). Mary Clifford expressed it thus:

5 Quoted in evidence to the *Royal Commission on the Aged Poor*, vol. 2, 6200
6 *ibid.*
7 *op. cit.,* 6216
8 *op. cit.,* 6208
9 Election address of George A. Gibbs, prospective Conservative candidate for Bristol West, 6 January 1906 in *Bristol Guardian* newspaper
10 Martin, *op. cit.* p. 169

I think that the only conclusion which I might state is, that it appears that in the case of Bristol, the thoroughly deserving and saving people do appear to have a large, possibly a sufficient provision made for them, out of those endowed charities, those annuities, and the large number of places in the almshouses, when you consider that nearly £5,000 is given away in annuities, and that there are 406 places in almshouses. It seems, if the best cases were uniformly admitted, as if there would be a very large provision for the really deserving pensions.[11]

What annoyed the likes of Clifford and many vicars of inner-city parishes was the lottery-like way doles, annuities and pensions were given out and the reluctance of charity trustees to explain the rationale behind decisions. When asked by the Commission on this matter, Mary Clifford was adamant that 'They are not distributed upon any principle whatsoever'.[12] She criticised the process of receiving annuities as a potential recipient had to enlist the help of a trustee to put the case forward and accused the endowed charities as a whole of preferring to take advice from 'their friends'. Unless this happened, there was no possibility of the case being brought forward she complained:

I imagine from the men who are the Charity Trustees that they would certainly satisfy themselves that the person was thoroughly respectable, and to some exent a proper applicant; but I must confess that there appears to be no system of discrimination between the cases; that if one was fortunate to obtain, for a case in which one was interested, the support of the president, that it would be possible that there would be other cases which would be investigated, but which might be even more deserving.[13]

Of course, we could get an insight into the method of the BMC with respect to care of the elderly were it not for the fact that the relevant minute books and almshouse registers for the period that the photographs cover are missing. This is unfortunate. The business in the general committee minutes are not in-depth enough to work out the process from application to success, or failure. The BMC Trustees meetings had a set formula for their meetings. Firstly, they dealt with cheque payments; then business left over from the last meeting; then new or renewed leases; and finally, payments under their charity scheme to individual almshouses or other business to do with the same, including admissions. So, for instance, we learn about the death of Joseph Lewis, a non-conformist aged 74 in Bengough's almshouse.[14] Almshouse residents had to be registered as either Church of England or non-conformist worshippers, which excluded Roman Catholics, other religions and probably the majority who could not really justify that they regularly practised any religion. Admission to one of their almshouses was invariably supplemented by allowances which ranged from seven to ten shillings per week. All in all, the BMC provided accomodation for 146 elderly out of a total provision of just over 400 for the city as a whole. Whilst applications to the Municipal Charity almshouses for this period do not survive, they do for the Lady Haberfield Almshouse Trust in Hotwells which had been founded in 1891 and was the most recent addition to Bristol's stock of almshouses as well as being a new, endowed charity. The type of applicant, and the rationale for admission, was fairly similar to the Municipal endowed almshouses. Haberfield was (and it still exists) an ecclesiastical, endowed charity which provided almshouse places for people in Redcliffe and Clifton. The surviving, pro-forma applications are the successful cases, although they include some who were eventually settled in other almshouses.[15]

11 *Royal Commission on the Aged Poor*, vol. 2, 6226

12 *op. cit.*, 6201

13 *op. cit.* 6190

14 BMC *Committee Minutes*, 23 February 1906

15 BRO/35717/I/3a

In 1903, William Hutchings was aged 60. He been a mariner for most of his working life, but had been forced to take the post of a night-watchman to support himself and applied on the grounds that his only surviving relative was his step-daughter and that he was, as he sorrowfully admitted, 'Practically alone in the world'. He was recommended as a 'first class case' by his main sponsor, the Bishop of Brechin.[16] All applications had to be supported initially by the vicar of St Mary Redcliffe for the places reserved for his parishioners, so it was inevitable that two criteria for acceptance were residence in the area and regular attendance at church.

Another case submitted to the Lady Haberfield trustees for consideration was that of Sarah Jane Mallard, a laundress, who had once had a small shop 'but did not find it answer well'. She had taken in washing all her life and when times were good had managed to earn between 14 and 15 shillings a week. Prior to eventually entering Redcliffe almshouse, these earnings had dropped to four shillings a week. Her husband was dead; she had three children, one of whom was a labourer in London (and therefore away) and a daughter who was named on the application form as being willing to pay for extra medical expenses should they ever become necessary (it is invariably a female named as being the next-of-kin responsible). Sarah felt she was '..now in too weak health to be able to get on with hard work — a son who would have been a help to me died a few years ago'.[17]

Taking on the responsibility of looking after an elderly relative, should their health deteriorate to an extent that the almshouse felt unable to look after them, was no idle promise. Eliza Norman, who had survived by letting lodgings all her life, was removed in an ambulance to her daughter at 19, Charlotte Street after suffering a paralytic stroke. She hung on for about seven months before dying at the daughter's home in December 1908.[18] Another female applicant, Henrietta Cantle, applied for admission in February 1904, but did not gain admittance until March 1906. She struggled on a Bonville annuity (a BMC eleemosynary fund) of £13 per annum, finding it impossible to exist on such a sum.[19] The delay in gaining entry was of concern to her vicar who referred to the case in a letter to the trustees in 1905, expressing his discontent that more pensions seemed to be going the way of Clifton residents, and reminded the board that at least half were for residents of his own parish. He ended his missive with the terse request that a revision of Mrs Cantle's position be considered 'and trust that there will be no hesitation on the part of the Trustees in filling up the vacancy with a Redcliffe tenant'.[20]

Most applicants relied on some sort of string pulling in order to get a place, the testimonials expanding on the worth of the individual's case. Ann Brown, a widow, who applied to enter Haberfield in 1910, aged 60 years of age, had been a domestic servant earning 5s. a week. She could provide letters of recommendation from the daughter of the household in which she had been a servant — 'I believe her to be Well Deserving'; from a manager in her husband's firm (he had been in charge of the Royal Insurance Company Fire Brigade) who remarked ' … *for she is a respectable and worthy woman, deserving help*'. Another had known her for 'very many years' and asked that 'I do hope you will try your best to get her into Lady Haberfield's Alms-House — Her working days are over — she has brought up her family of 7 right well — and is really most deserving'.[21] Although Mrs Brown gained admission, the outcome for most people, despite their merit, could be a like a 'lucky dip'. The vicar of St Mary Redcliffe, in one letter accompanying a batch of application forms to the trustees, appended, without any rationale, a list of his parishioners in

16 BRO/35717/I/31
17 *op. cit.,* /33
18 *op. cit.,* /32
19 *ibid.*
20 *op. cit.,* letter, 6 January 1906
21 *op. cit.,* /37

order of merit, but with rider that, 'They are all most worthy'.

To a degree, this confirms the general opinion of opponents of endowed charity care for the elderly that its distribution was irrational. One of the problems in relying on testimony from sources created by critics, however, is that all were prejudiced against these historic, endowed charities. In the margin of the BMC's own copy of the printed Royal Commission report on the elderly are plenty of comments about the accuracy of accusations made about their procedures. The comment 'Wrong!' is inserted in the margin against a section which made reference to the fact that many of the annuities were for freemen of the old city or their wives, or limited to non-paupers. The accuser quoted Thurston's charity as an example; but in fact, this was a lying-in charity, and was one of the endowments that really was for the poor. In 1906, the Charities were approached by the Corporation's Town Clerk who asked them if they would reconsider how Alderman Kitchen's endowment might be distributed to meet the needs of the poor. The trustees responded with the fact that they had to be mindful of the original donor's bequest, but that they continually made changes to meet prevailing circumstances and that much of the fund in this instance was going to meet the needs of such people anyway.[22] Nevertheless, the outcome was that much benefit went on those who had once been financially secure, but had fallen on hard times, rather than help those who had permanently been in the pauper trap. The restriction that probably ensured this always remained the case was that most applicants for annuities should not have been receiving poor relief prior to making their application. This is confirmed by the Haberfield applications. Not one had ever received poor relief, and often the statement 'Never' is found against the question, emphasising perhaps the indignity some individuals felt about even being asked if they had ever resorted to such a mechanism for support.

Relations between the endowed charities in Bristol with voluntary and local authority provision was, as we have gathered from the statements of critics to date, strained. By 1906, the situation was improving. Some co-operation between Guardians and charities under the Charity Organisation Society was formed in which the Poor Law board agreed to provide information to charitable agencies and four Guardians were appointed to the board of the Council of the Civic League.[23] Two years later, in 1908, the Old Age Pension Act gave five shillings a week for the first time to some pensioners aged 70 or over, although it initially disqualified those who had received poor relief in the previous year. As a consequence of O.A.Ps. getting these pensions, which were administered by Pensions Committees, the BMC reduced almshouse pay so that combined income for any almshouse person would not exceed 10 shillings (15 shillings in the case of married couples) and cut the amount paid to individuals receiving annuities. They also decided that, 'special cases excepted', to remove 'elderly brethren and sisters' on reaching the age of 70 from their almshouses.[24] The new pension arrangement, radical though the concept might be, could also be a disruptive influence on old people's lives.

22 BMC *Committee Minutes, 2 February* 1906
23 Martin *op. cit.*, p. 163
24 BMC *Miscellaneous Minute Book*, p. 93

The Photographs
Bristol in 1906

Bristol in 1906

These photographs represent a prime example of the change that happens to documentary sources over time; that is, although they were created for one purpose, the ever-growing distance between then and now has given them another. They have become historical evidence.

The photographs were taken to give the Bristol Municipal Charities a convenient pictorial record of their city properties at that time. As an administrative tool they must have been very useful to the BMC surveyor, Frank Wills, who could refer to them, along with two plan books created at roughly the same time, as a visual *aide-memoire* of the property portfolio under his care. However, the passage of time has given them a new significance: they show us a city at a pivotal point in our history, on the cusp between the Victorian age and the rapid changes wrought in the twentieth century. We are seeing Bristol and Bristolians before two world wars took their toll of both of them.

What do these photographs show us? Many buildings that have fallen to bombs and re-development; but also many buildings that are still with us, though often standing in an entirely new environment. We see people going about their business: working, shopping, playing, or just standing around. We see the modern age on the horizon: motor garages are beginning to appear; but the old is still very much to the fore: there is actually no sign of any motor vehicle in these photographs and all carrying seems to be done by hand cart and horse-drawn transport (the amount of horse dung in the road on nearly every picture testifies to the ubiquity of the horse). We see that people wrote graffiti on walls as they have always done, but also that children often used walls as focal points for their games. We see how fashions have changed: girls in pinafores, boys in caps and Eton collars, men and women all wearing hats, old ladies in black bombazine, and the clothes generally, without the benefit of new fibres, seeming thick and unwieldy. Finally, we see how indomitable is our will to brighten up our surroundings: witness the number of window boxes and pots of plants in these streets where gardens have mostly been sacrificed to provide extra accommodation and work-space.

What aren't we getting from these photographs? We are not, on the whole, seeing squalor. Most of the people in the pictures are above the poverty line (if only just above in some cases), and the BMC were most certainly not slum landlords, so none of their properties are in a really decayed state, unless they are vacant and awaiting refurbishment. We are not seeing the *scale* of the properties. With the exception of large warehouses it should be born in mind that most of these buildings are very small (often long and narrow thus betraying their ancient origin). To exemplify this, look at photograph 54. The pub at No. 29 Old Market Street still exists (now the Old Market Tavern), but it has been joined with the property next door, known as The Don in the picture, to make one reasonably-sized (but not massive) pub. The original Bunch of Grapes must have been tiny. Similarly, compare the size of the actual Upper Berkeley Place with the seemingly open, spacious haven shown in photograph 18. The camera, then, even when trying to create a dispassionate factual record, is to some extent misleading us; perhaps this is the result of the lenses employed at the time.

We are not seeing the new Edwardian Bristol with its growing suburbs; we are only walking about the old city where time may not have stood still exactly (it was still a vibrant business and commercial centre), but certainly where various constraints, legal and geographical, had meant that much of it still retained its ancient look.

The photographs have been arranged, as far as is possible, to match the order in which the BMC schedules of properties were arranged; that is, generally in alphabetical order by street. Indeed, although the photographs in the two albums themselves are not in perfect order, it seems clear that this is what had been originally intended. This will hopefully make it easy for students to work from the schedules to the photographs if they wish to pursue and extend the work begun in this book. The schools and almshouses have been placed at the beginning, since it was these that the properties were intended to support via their individual charities (for a list of the properties by charity, see appendix 2). Again, this seems to be in accordance with BMC practice. There is not a picture of every property owned; for instance, a photograph of some buildings in Old Market Street has clearly been removed from the album, and one or two properties owned at the time seem to have slipped the net (possibly the photographer occasionally found himself unable to find a good angle from which to shoot given the cramped state of much of the old city). However, the majority of the BMC's city property in 1906 is here, and what a fascinating study it makes.

Please use the maps supplied to locate the properties and put them into context; and above all, in studying the photographs, look for the small detail. It is in the small detail that we can really see our forbears; and though much may have changed, as the century closes we can look back to its beginning and share our common humanity.

Bristol Grammar School, Tyndall's Park. Built by Foster and Wood between 1875 and 1879.

In 1532 Robert Thorne, a Bristol merchant, obtained the estates of St. Bartholomew's Hospital, near the bottom of Christmas Steps (see photograph 22), in order to convey them to the Corporation (forerunner of the City Council) for the maintenance of a free grammar school. It was housed down in Christmas Street until 1767 when the Corporation decided that it would swap the premises of the Grammar School with those of Queen Elizabeth's Hospital in Unity Street, thus placing the poor and orphaned children of QEH in fairly unpleasant surroundings down in the fetor of the old city, whilst giving the better-off day boys a relatively new and spacious building near the light and air of College Green and the fashionable area around Park Street. It has been suggested that the motive was a little skulduggery perpetrated by Alderman Dampier on behalf of his imminent son-in-law, the headmaster of the Grammar School, in order to enhance the latter's status.

The school was managed by the Corporation until the reforms of the 1835 Municipal Corporations Act, when it was handed over to the Municipal Charity Trustees. It was in a poor state, having only been prepared to admit private boarders for some years. The Trustees set about bringing the school back to life, re-opening it in 1848 with between 200 and 300 boys.

It moved to the premises shown in the photograph in 1879, on a spacious site of six acres on the Clifton side of Tyndall's Park. By 1906 it was taking 400 boys, who were given the choice of a classical or a commercial and scientific training. The aim seems to have been to prepare boys for Oxford and Cambridge, the Military, the Home Civil Service, or business. [1]

Queen Elizabeth's Hospital, Berkeley Place. Looking from the bottom of Lower Clifton Hill across the roofs of Hill's Almshouse and Berkeley Place National School with Jacob's Wells Road beyond, towards Brandon Hill, with Cabot tower in the background to the right.

In his will of 1586, John Carr, a wealthy soap-maker, left property in Congresbury to provide for an 'hospital or place for bringing up of poor children and orphans, being men children'.

It was to be modelled on Christ's Hospital in London and the Corporation was to act as its governing body. It was opened in 1590 behind St. Mark's church in the mansion house and orchard that had once been part of Gaunt's Hospital. The school was rebuilt in 1702 and taken over by the Grammar School around 65 years later, when the boys of the City School, as QEH was also known, were moved down to the old Grammar School premises at Christmas Street, it being said that their present building was much too big for them.

In 1847 the school moved to the new Tudor-style building pictured here in its four acre site over a former Jewish cemetery on the north western side of Brandon Hill. Reliant as it was on income from its estates outside the city, the fall in agricultural rents of the last quarter of the nineteenth century meant that the school was short of funds, and the grand scheme of housing three schools in the building was unrealised, as was the full compliment of 160 boy boarders (there were 127 in 1906).

Their uniform consisted of an ankle-length blue coat, knee-breeches and orange stockings. On their heads they wore a blue cap with an orange band around it and bob of the same colour. [2]

Red Maids' School, Denmark Street. We are looking south east down Denmark Street towards St. Augustine's Parade from the front of Protheroe's warehouse (see photographs 25-6). In the foreground are the premises of Harveys, the wine merchants, and beyond them Red Maids' School, under which Harveys rented a cellar from the BMC.

The school was founded by Alderman John Whitson who, by his will of 1627, bequeathed property to the Mayor and Commonalty of Bristol in order to provide for forty poor girls, daughters of freemen* who were either dead or fallen on hard times. The girls were to be taught to read, to sew, and do work towards their keep. The building in the picture was built in 1840 on part of the Gaunt's Hospital site, and housed eighty girls, all boarders. The subjects taught were equivalent to those at other schools, with the addition of 'domestic economy, the laws of health, needlework, and some skilled industry suitable for women' (Arrowsmith's *Dictionary of Bristol*, 1906). At this time the majority of pupils were those who had lost one or both parents, or whose parents could not maintain them, and they wore red, with white aprons and tippets, and plain straw bonnets trimmed with blue ribbon. A sum of £50 was annually put aside to enable the provision of marriage portions (dowries) to girls who had left the school. The school moved to its present site in Westbury on Trym in 1911.

* Those who had attained the freedom of the city and could thus vote at parliamentary elections like the freeholders. **[3]**

Trinity Hospital North, Old Market Street. Looking down the long narrow courtyard, flanked on both sides by dwellings, which led off from the north side of Old Market Street, to the left of the buildings shown in photograph 55 and 57 (the buildings to the right were parallel to Barcroft Place, which was just behind them).

It has been suggested that this almshouse partner to Trinity Hospital South (see below), was founded by John Barstaple's wife, Isabella, though there seems to be no actual evidence to support this. It was at first used to house poor travellers to and from Bristol for up to three nights (both north and south establishments were just inside Lawford's Gate, the eastern entrance to the city). However it was closed in the uncertain times of the first half of the sixteenth century and leased out for other uses, and it was not until 1672 that it was recovered, rebuilt, and put to use providing proper homes for the poor (twelve widows were admitted).

Having been extended in 1730, the premises seen in this picture remained until 1913 when they were replaced by the buildings which can still be seen today. The new almshouse was provided by the chairman of the Trustees of the Bristol Municipal Charities at the time, Fenwick Richards.

At the time of this photograph, there were twenty four inmates mainly of 60 years of age and over, each receiving a weekly allowance of 7 shillings. The new premises extended only down the western (left-hand) side of the site, and must have been lighter and airier, but as a result the number of inmates that could be accommodated was cut by half.   [4]

Trinity Hospital South, Old Market Street. We are looking along the western wing of the almshouse, across the top of Old Market Street towards Trinity Hospital North.

Founded by John Barstaple, a wealthy merchant, in the late fourteenth century, it was intended that it provide twelve chambers and twelve gardens for six poor men and six poor women, with a priest to officiate in its own chapel. Further bequests were made to it over the centuries that followed, both in terms of money and properties by which to generate income.

Though it is hard to visualise now, the alms-

house occupies a site which originally was raised up (land behind the buildings was known as 'the Batch', indicating this), giving the inmates pleasant views over open countryside from just inside Bristol's walls at Lawford's Gate.

The building was rebuilt in 1857-8, and further additions were made throughout the latter half of the nineteenth century, culminating in the re-erection of the chapel in 1882, complete with time-capsule of local papers and a history of the institution lodged in its foundation stone. In style these new buildings were an example of the BMC architects'(Foster and Wood), fairy-tale confections of the Tudor, with its half-timbering etc., embellished by the tracery, crocketing (little figures running up and down the roofs) and patterned brickwork of the French (Burgundian) Gothic.   [5]

Trinity Hospital South, Old Market Street. We are looking along the western wing from the main gate on Old Market Street. Running behind these buildings is Midland Road (see photograph 47).

There were difficult times during the upheavals of the seventeenth century: the hospital's money often went on pensions for poor people not living-in; the building was managed by a light-fingered bailiff; and it was thought necessary to make inmates comply with rules, the breaking of which could lead to fines or expulsion, the latter being the punishment if inmates married after being admitted to the almshouse.

The eighteenth century saw the Dial Almshouse, as the hospital was also known, having a complement of ten men, ten women, a bedmaker and a washerwoman. By 1906, thanks particularly to the rebuilding and expansion of the hospital in the late nineteenth century, there were four men and thirty two women, all over 60 years of age, living there. The inmates' weekly allowance rose from 4 shillings in 1822 to 7 shillings in 1880 (the same sum they were receiving when this photograph was taken).

The 1891 Census shows that the inmates were not necessarily Bristolians by birth: out of thirty four listed, only twelve were born in Bristol, the rest most commonly naming Gloucestershire, Somerset, Wiltshire, Devon and South Wales as their birthplaces, with one being from the Black Forest in Germany. This of course has no bearing on qualification for entrance, since one only needed to have lived in Bristol for three years and not claimed poor relief during that period, but it does tell us something of the drawing-power of a big city upon its region, in terms of the search for employment that probably brought most of these people or their families to Bristol originally.

Incidentally, following its rebuilding from 1857- 82, the building is referred to on this Census as the 'New Trinity Alms House'. [6]

Trinity Hospital South, Old Market Street. A close-up of Foster and Wood's magnificent almshouse, allowing us to enjoy their unflagging attention to detail. Their skill in creating an environment which somehow seems to involve the onlooker with its surprises, big and small, round every corner and at every level, from roof to floor, has been a source of pleasure since they were built, and - remains so today. [7]

Foster's Almshouse, Colston Street. On the corner of Colston Street and Christmas Steps.

This establishment was founded by John Foster between 1481 and 1483. It was built on Steep Street, along with a chapel dedicated to the Three Kings of Cologne in which Foster intended that a priest should sing for his soul, the soul of his late wife, and of both their families, once he had died. The almshouse was to contain no-one who was not English, and no-one was to be under 50 years of age or married. His executor, John Esterfield, made further bequests to the benefit of the almshouse, and stipulated that four of the women admitted should be nominated by the Mayoress of Bristol.

Steep Street was, as its name suggests, hard going. It was narrow too, and G.F. Stone, in his *Bristol: As It Was — And As It Is* (1909), tells us that, being amazingly on the main route from Bristol to Wales, with the mail-coaches making their way up and down it, the upper storey of one of the over-hanging old houses had to be chamfered off to let them pass freely. However this was to change in 1861 when the BMC Trustees decided to rebuild Foster's Almshouse. The project took until 1883 to complete, by which time Steep Street had given way to the wider and more convenient Colston Street. The new almshouse was the fascinating Hollywood film-set of a building seen here. It is patterned by bricks supplied by the Cattybrook Brick Co. of Almondsbury, and, like Trinity Hospital South, it is a monument of Foster and Wood's idiosyncratic Burgundian Gothic (described by Latimer in his *Annals of Bristol* (1887) as, '...praiseworthy, in spite of some meretricious details of a continental character', and well worth taking the time to appreciate, since no detail seems to have been too small for the coincidentally-named architect, John Foster, to have considered.

To the left of the picture is the chapel of the Three Kings of Cologne, which was modified by Foster and Wood at the same time.

In 1906 Foster's Almshouse contained twenty-eight inmates of both sexes over the age of 60, four women still chosen by the Lady Mayoress. Each received 7 shillings per week. **[8]**

(Opposite page): **Alderman Stevens' Almshouse, Old Market Street.** This was situated about three-quarters of the way along the north side of Old Market Street towards Lawford's Gate (see photograph 54). It was not owned or administered by the BMC, but they did own the site, it being one of Trinity Hospital's portfolio of properties. The almshouse itself was the concern of the Feoffees of Thomas Stevens.

It was founded by Alderman Stevens (Steevens), who by his will of 1679 gave lands and tenements in Bridge Yate and Wick and Abson, to the east of Bristol, as a means to buy two sites, one in the parish of St. Philip and Jacob and one in that of Temple, for the erection of two almshouses, each to contain twelve poor men and women. A piece of land was bought in Old Market Street from the Feoffees of Trinity Hospital, and the almshouse was built in 1686 for the housing of freemen's widows or daughters. The other almshouse was built in Temple Street, but was demolished in 1872 to make way for the new Victoria Street. Its inmates were moved to the Old Market premises which were enlarged to take them. In the early years of this century, around when this photograph was taken, there were twenty four inmates, each receiving 7 or 8 shillings per week.

The building in the picture is presumed to have been built in 1725, since this is the date carved with the bust of Alderman Stevens at the far end of the court seen here. Sadly this almshouse has now gone, the site being occupied by a fairly recent building, Steevens House. **[9]**

Bengough's Almshouse, Horfield Road. This was founded by Henry Bengough, who by his will of 1818, left property in the North Somerset parishes of Nempnett Thrubwell and Blagdon to provide the means for the building and subsistence of a hospital next to Trinity Hospital for aged men and women (not under 59 years of age). The inmates should be in the proportion of two women to one man, half to be Church of England and half Protestant Dissenters.

There were not sufficient funds to build the almshouse until 1877, and by then there was no suitable site near Trinity Hospital, so finally Bengough's Almshouse was built (by Foster and Wood) just to the north east of Colston's Almshouse on Horfield Road in 1878. The two foundations Colston's* and Bengough's are very close together, with only Colston Villa (see photograph 35) between the back of the former and the front of the latter. Nowadays Bengough's Almshouse looks down over the Bristol Oncology Centre which is across Horfield Road from it.

In 1906 there were eighteen married couples receiving ten shillings per week, and two single women receiving 7 shillings per week. Like Foster's and Trinity Almshouses, applicants need only have lived in Bristol for three years and not received poor relief in that time.

Interestingly, on the night that the 1891 Census was taken, one couple, Mr. and Mrs. Burt (80 and 78 respectively), had their unmarried 47 year-old daughter, Emma, staying with them. She is described as a 'worsted winder' by occupation. Mr. and Mrs. Burt, in common with two other couples, occupied three rooms rather than the more usual two. Perhaps Emma was a permanent resident?   [10]

*Colston's Almshouse is the responsibility of the Society of Merchant Venturers, not the BMC.

Ash Lodge, Temple. Ash Lodge was in fact a passageway which led from Temple Back (see photograph 91), to the south eastern end of Temple churchyard. The potteries, foundries and other fairly heavy industry of the area crowded in on it.

The 1891 Census gives an impression of a large number of very small houses, all crammed in together, but by 1906, when these pictures were taken, a certain amount of rationalisation seems to have taken place. The BMC owned six 'cottages', all but one of which being kept vacant on the advice of their surveyor, Frank Wills, who thought that the 'migratory' type of tenant which they attracted too much trouble for too little return.

Shortly after this, these buildings were demolished to provide a store, and in 1912 the BMC submitted plans for a warehouse on the site.   [11]

Ash Lodge, Temple. The origin of the name 'Ash Lodge' is hard to discover. Bristol's Land Tax assessments (to be found at Bristol Record Office) show that in the eighteenth century the area was known as 'Grumblers Ash' up until 1759, when it became 'Ash Lodge'. Perhaps 'Grumblers Ash' was a corruption of 'Grumbald's Ash', the Gloucestershire hundred* just to the north of Bristol. However, the 'lodge' at present remains a mystery, as does the reason for the transference of Gloucestershire place-name to Bristol.

The cottage shown here seems to be inhabited, if the net curtain at the window is any indication. This would make it No. 6, the only tenanted cottage at the time, leased to James Knott.   [12]

*Counties were divided into 'hundreds' each with its own court. By the nineteenth century they had been superseded by other, more recognisable authorities, such as the district councils).

Ash Lodge, Temple. In the high wall shown here can be seen evidence that dwellings have been demolished. In the nineteenth century, as the 1891 Census shows, this area must have been fairly densely populated. In the little houses lived labourers, cap makers, pipe makers, a box maker, a slipper maker, a pottery furnace stoker, a bargeman, a foreman in an oil store, a veneer sawyer, a freestone cutter, corn porters on the docks, and their families. None of these would have to have walked far from their front doors to work, living as they did, in an area abounding in potteries and other industries, all close to the Floating Harbour.   [13]

Nos. 1-5 Barrs Street. Looking up the east side of Barrs Street from Old King Street, with Ridley's Almshouse ('for 5 bachelors and 5 maids') on its corner with Milk Street. On the opposite corner is the *Plume of Feathers* public house, with the Milk Street sign attached to it.

At No.1 Barrs Street is William George Radford, saddler and harness maker, and next to him, at No. 2, with a large sign projecting from the property, Philip Nash, bespoke shoe maker. At Nos. 3, 4 and 5, are a furniture dealer (Mrs I.M. Stockman), a refreshment house, and a fruiterer, respectively.

Barrs Street ran from somewhere near the northern end of modern Merchant Street to the eastern (Bond Street) end of the St. James Barton roundabout/subway, by Avon House North. The name *Barr's Court* remains to remind us. [14]

Nos. 8-12 Barrs Street. Looking up the east side of Barrs Street towards St. James Barton this time, at Frank Bound's tobacconist and newsagent's shop (No. 9). Next door are Willey and Co., timber merchants, and in the tall building (No. 11), Albert Crookes, cutler and grinder. No. 12, just before Scully the printer, seems to have contained a variety of people: Mrs E. Fowler, a hairdresser; F.I. Rogers; John Henry Godfrey, a carpenter; James Winchester, a coach builder; and Henry Colston Reeves, a chair maker. All this in a shop, dwelling house and two cottages in the rear.

Outside the newsagent's shop the headlines are as follows: *Daily Mail,* 'Church Ritual Great Reforms Proposed'; *Daily Express,* 'Are Church Collections Illegal?'. [15]

Nos. 13-15 Barrs Street. Looking down the east side of Barrs Street, from its junction with St. James Barton towards the shops seen in photograph 15. Nearest us, on the corner, is Charles Fisher and Co., wine and spirit merchants, having a 'dwelling house, wine cellar, warehouse and offices, with yard in rear, two stables, coach-houses and shed' (so says the BMC schedule of its properties).

Next, at No. 14, are Hall and Pedder, lamp manufacturers, and next again, at No. 13, Joseph Scully, printer and bookbinder. Just to the left of the picture part of the roof of the Y.M.C.A. building in St. James' Square. [16]

Nos. 27, 29, 31 Berkeley Place, Clifton. Berkeley Place joins the steep road on the western side of Brandon Hill, which begins as Jacobs Wells Road, to the Triangle. To the right of the picture is the entrance to Queen Elizabeth's Hospital. Next to it, at No. 31, are the premises of A. Bendall and Sons, chimney sweeps (the BMC's official sweeps), and then, going up the hill, David Morgan, smith, gas fitter and plumber, and Alfred Ernest Ball, upholsterer. Both Nos. 27 and 29 had gardens at the rear, but Mr. Bendall had a cottage, wash house and shed behind his premises. The site of Mr. Bendall's premises is now occupied by the QEH theatre. [17]

Nos. 9 & 10 Upper Berkeley Place. At the south western corner of the Triangle, these attractive houses, forming the base to another, smaller triangle, were designed by Thomas Paty and Sons, who were responsible for a great deal of the elegance of Bristol's Georgian architecture. We are looking south towards the highest point of the site, behind which are the grounds of Queen Elizabeth's Hospital and the north western slopes of Brandon Hill. These houses are still standing, though the trees in the centre are now mature, as might be expected, giving the place a much more enclosed air. Sadly the houses which once filled the north western side of the little triangle (out of shot to the right of the picture) are now gone. In 1906 William Quance lived at No. 9 and Robert Jackson, headmaster of Queen Elizabeth's Hospital (otherwise known as the City School), lived at No. 10 (on the end, to the left).

As one might expect given the relative (middle-class) opulence of the area (look no further than the proudly displayed aspidistra in the window of the second house from the left, No. 9), the children in the foreground seem better dressed than most of those seen in the other photographs in this collection. Behind them sits a goat, tethered there, perhaps, to keep the grass down. [18]

No. 1 Christmas Steps. A familiar view, even to us today, of the buildings at the bottom of Christmas Steps (see also photograph 22), looking from Christmas Street towards Host Street. To the left of the picture, nearest us, is the shop of Charles George Earl, watchmaker. No. 1 Christmas Steps is on the corner of Host Street and Christmas Steps, in the middle of the picture, the sign stretching from shop front to roof advertising 'Ashcroft & Co., Pure Family Bread'. It was leased to Spillers and Bakers Ltd., who had flour mills on Redcliffe Back (and whose successors are still milling today at Avonmouth). Wright's 1906 Directory lists Joseph Harry Lock as the occupant. [20]

No. 42 Broadmead. We are looking down the south side of Broadmead towards Merchant Street. On the corner is the Rose and Crown. The BMC owned No. 42 (with its sun-awning down) at which was the furniture warehouse of John Thomas Wright and Co., here advertising 'mattresses re-made' and 'spring cleaning'. In the following year these premises were taken over by Edward Miles, the bacon curer, seen next door at No. 43, which had also been leased by Wright until recently. Just out of shot, to the right of the picture, is the Greyhound Hotel, the facade of which is still there today, acting as an entrance to the Galleries shopping complex.

Not a BMC property, to the left of Wright's premises are Masters' Princess Royal Dining and Supper Rooms, somehow giving a flavour of the era through their title. **[19]**

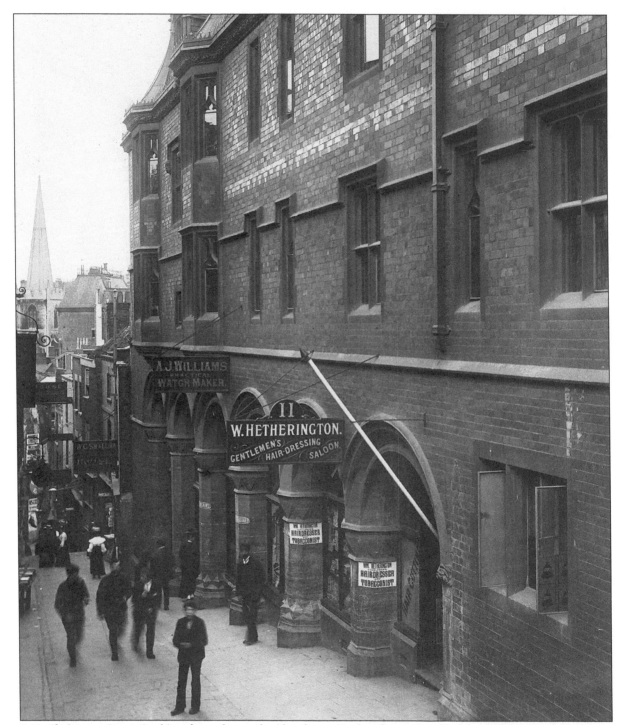

9-11 Christmas Steps. Looking down the south side of Christmas Steps at a group of shops which are part of the Foster's Almshouses complex, their ground floors having been given an arcade effect in keeping with Foster and Wood's historical theme. We are just below the sixteenth century Chapel of the Three Kings of Cologne which is at the top of the Steps, where they meet Colston Street. In the distance is the tower of St. John the Baptist church, now all but obscured from this angle by an office block.

Furthest from us is at No. 9, but with no sign visible, is John King, furniture dealer; next up the hill at No. 10 is Alfred J. Williams, watchmaker; nearest us, clearly at No. 11, is William Hetherington's 'gentlemen's hairdressing saloon'. The posters pasted to the columns outside his shop indicate that he considered himself a tobacconist as well — probably quite a lucrative side-line for someone with an all-male clientele in an era when most men smoked. **[21]**

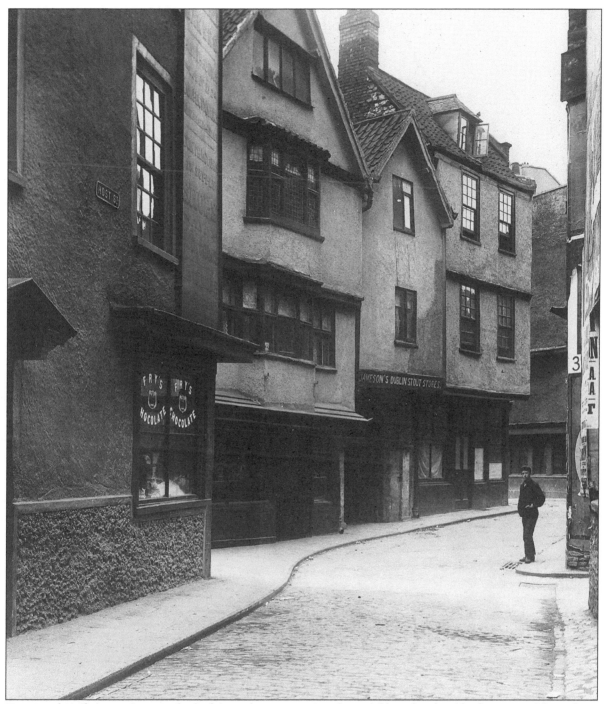

Nos. 17 and 19 Christmas Street. A clutch of sixteenth century buildings where Christmas Street and Host Street meet at the foot of Christmas Steps. At No. 17, just recently moved from round the corner on Christmas Steps, is John Besser's fish and chip shop (until very recently occupied by Edwin Hand, greengrocer and pork butcher), and next door to the right, Watkins, Jameson, Pim and Co. Ltd., brewers (Dublin). The brewery was accessed via the gateway to St. Bartholomew's Hospital, underneath the sign saying 'Jameson's Dublin Stout Stores'. Just visible on the other side of Narrow Lewin's Mead, just behind the onlooker, is Willway's Dye Works and Laundry Co. Ltd., also BMC tenants (see photograph 23).

Interestingly, No. 17 is still a fish and chip shop today. The medieval St. Bartholomew's Hospital was used by two of the charities administered by the BMC over the years: it housed the Bristol Grammar School in 1532, and the City School (Queen Elizabeth's Hospital) in 1766.

[22]

Christmas Street, Willway's Dye Works. On the southern tip of an island of buildings formed by Christmas Street (down which the worried-looking boy is marching towards us), Narrow Lewin's Mead (which runs between the buildings to the left, where the lady and gentleman have paused to look at the cameraman), and Rupert Street (which runs off to the right). A little further down Rupert Street (part of this island), could be found the paper warehouse and Oddfellows' Hall shown in photograph 85. To the extreme left can be seen the edge of Jameson's Dublin Stout Stores, one of the old buildings at the bottom of Christmas Steps to be seen in photographs 20 and 22.

The building directly in front of us is occupied by Willway's Dye Works and Laundry Co. Ltd. It also acts as a bill-posting station, as can clearly be seen. Bill posters like Billing Jarrett, Read and Co. Ltd. could expect to pay the BMC anything from £1-2 per year for the use of such a space.

The Princes Theatre has obviously splashed out to advertise its latest production, *The Spring Chicken,* and the *Christian Banner* is keen to grab a readership for its first issue, 'ready April 26th'. …Red Cross Blue is a sign of another era, before biological washing powders, when people would put 'laundress's blue' into their whites wash to give the finished product an illusion of whiteness. The wall behind advertises GWR Easter excursions.

[23]

No. 49 Corn Street. The heart of Bristol's business and financial district. This is the corner of Corn Street and Small Street, opposite the Corn Exchange. The ground floor is clearly occupied by Thomas Cook and Son, tourist excursion and passenger shipping offices. Above them is William Henry Brown, solicitor. **[24]**

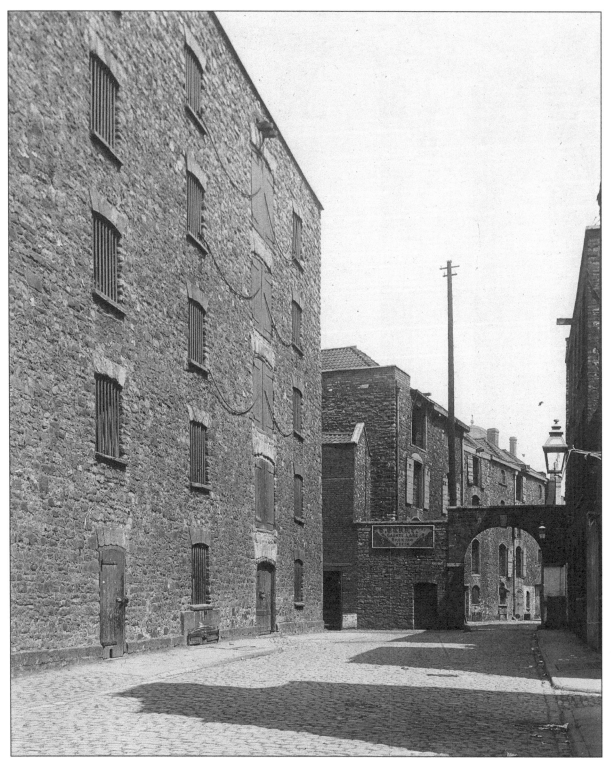

Denmark Street/Gaunt's Lane, Protheroe's Warehouse. Still there today, a huge block of warehouses with cellars fronting onto Denmark Street, surrounded by Gaunt's Lane (seen here) to the south east, Orchard Lane (seen to the left disappearing behind the building) on the north east, and Hobbs' Lane on the north west. Through the archway was St. Augustine's Hall (another warehouse), now refurbished as offices. The sign at the end of the lane advertises S. Berry's shoeing forge, a vital service in an area of warehouses when just about all carrying was done by horse power. [25]

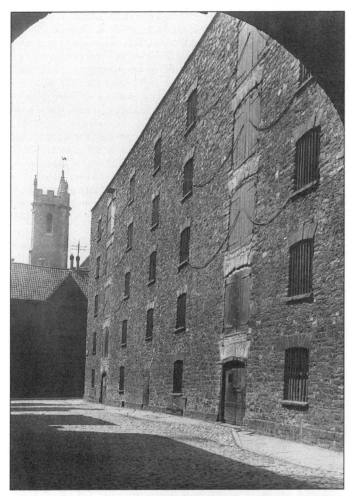

Denmark Street/Gaunt's Lane, Protheroe's Warehouse. The same property as in photograph 25, but this time we are looking from the gateway seen in that picture (the access to St. Augustine's Hall), down Gaunt's Lane towards Denmark Street and the premises of John Harvey and Sons, the wine merchants. In the background is the red tower of St. Mark's Church (the Lord Mayor's Chapel).

Protheroe's warehouse (which may also have been known as Denmark Street Hall) was leased to Ford and Canning, bonded warehouse keepers, who also occupied St. Augustine's Hall (see photograph 58), King Street Hall, and traded as coopers and cask dealers on The Grove. [26]

Nos. 25-31 Ellbroad Street, St. Matthias. Ellbroad Street ran between Broad Weir to the north west and Redcross Street to the south east, very much in a working-class industrial area of the city. At one end was Adlam's foundry and at the other, the Redcross Street Tannery (see photograph 80). Its site has been obliterated by Bond Street, just to the north of where it meets Old Market Street.

To the right is the house of Samuel Shewring (designated a shopkeeper and spelled 'Showering' in Wright's 1906 Directory), who also had a workshop behind his house which may have been the place of business of Thomas Wreford, a wood carver. Mr. Shewring was obviously keen to brighten his environment, judging by the number of plant pots on his upstairs window sills and over his front door. Next door, at No. 29, we can see the sign of the Crown Printing Works, run by George Fear. Next to this (No. 27) is Emma Carter, then the entrance to Ellsbridge Passage, over which Charles Luxton, cooper, has been permitted (at an annual rent of 6d.) to hang his signboard. The shop window beyond belongs to Mrs Elizabeth Seaford's grocery store (No. 25). [27]

Ellsbridge Passage, Ellbroad Street, St. Matthias. Ellsbridge Passage snaked its long and narrow way north from Ellbroad Street to Victoria Road/Ropewalk, emerging as a slim alley alongside the Three Horse Shoes public house (see photograph 80). It consisted of something like seven cottages and four or five workshops, along with three wash-houses. Only two w.c.'s (and these shared) are mentioned in the BMC's survey of the period. It is now under the Haberfield multi-storey car park, where Bond Street meets Wellington Road.

We are looking up the passage, from the Ellbroad Street end towards Victoria Road/Ropewalk and the Three Horse Shoes. The photograph does not show us as grim a scene as one might expect, but given its cramped conditions and probable lack of light in places, it cannot have been too pleasant a place to live. At least, unlike many courts, it was accessible from both sides and not a dead end. [28]

Ellsbridge Passage, Ellbroad Street, St. Matthias. Looking at an angle from the Victoria Road/Ropewalk end across at the cottages seen in photograph 28.

The BMC lists the tenants as follows: William Everton, George Jenkins, George Briggs, George Haynes, Ada Francis, Emma Owen, Charles Luxton (we know from his sign on Ellbroad Street that he had a workshop here).

The 1891 Census shows households of four to six members, with the occasional lodger (the exception being No. 7, which, in addition to a family of four, also contained a family of six as lodgers). Occupations are listed as coffee roaster, washer woman, milliner, tailoress, french polisher, nurse, grocer's porter, errand boy, cab driver, dress maker, and there are general labourers as well. The only 1906 tenant who was there in 1891 was George Briggs, who lived at No. 4. He was a french polisher, aged 49 in 1891, and he lived there with his wife and four sons. [29]

Ellsbridge Passage, Ellbroad Street, St. Matthias. Looking across the passage from someone's lawn/animal enclosure(?) at some of the workshops and wash-houses of the passage. The buildings beyond might belong to Adlam's foundry.

Ellsbridge (or Ellbridge) Passage led to and from a small bridge (Ell Bridge, perhaps; an ell being an old measurement of length and thus indicating the span of the bridge) which crossed the River Frome at Narrow Weir next to the Three Horeshoes (see photograph 80), before it was covered in the nineteenth century. **[30]**

Frogmore Street, Denmark Avenue. Looking down Denmark Avenue towards the Hatchet Inn on Frogmore Street. The photographer is actually interested in the building on the right (the Frogmore Street-side of which can be seen on photograph 32), but obviously couldn't resist the seventeenth century glory of the Hatchet. (Miss S.E.M. Loveridge, landlady).

The fairly new BMC property to the right of the picture was leased to Frederick Wallis Stoddart, who at the time was the city's public analyst.

The newspaper headlines outside Miss Eliza Hugh's newsagent's shop announce 'Gun accident near Plymouth: Gloucester Volunteers Injured' and 'The Studio Tragedy in London: Evidence at the Inquest Verdict'. Local history, too, was obviously catered for even then, 'Lundy Island a Century Ago'. **[31]**

Nos. 22-30 Frogmore Street. A glorious sunny view up Frogmore Street, from just below the Hatchet towards Trenchard Street and the Colston Hall. All the BMC properties are on the right hand side: No.22, a warehouse and tenement occupied by William Burns, is just beyond the woman with the baby and two girls; then, at No. 24, 26 and 28 are the stables, coach-house, van-house and warehouses leased by F. Burman and Son. This company is designated 'french polishers' in Wright's 1906 directory, but it is clear from their signboard that they considered another of their areas of activity to be more important: 'Removal Contractors by Road, Rail or Sea'. At No. 30, a sign just visible, is Thomas E. Wookey's furniture repository. **[32]**

Nos. 32 & 40 Frogmore Street. Approaching the top of Frogmore Street. Nearest us, at No. 32, lived William Barry; then, at No. 40, last building but one before the corner with Pipe Lane, Mrs Ellen Fitzgerald had her greengrocer's shop. Between the two, builders seem to be erecting a new building beneath the signboard of Samuel Martin and Son, carpenter, builder and undertaker. Perhaps it is indeed Samuel Martin and Son.

No. 32 presents a rather continental scene, with its upper window thrown open and its small balcony, with a bird cage hanging from it, filled by plant pots and a dog sunning itself! [**33**]

Nos. 5-7 Guinea Street, Redcliffe. The street runs from Redcliffe Hill on the east, past the entrance to the General Hospital, to Bathurst Basin on the west. This shows the north side of the Redcliffe Hill end, just along from the Redcliffe Clergy House, where at the time the curates from St. Mary Redcliffe lived. Nos. 5-7 were built by the noted plasterer Joseph Thomas in 1740. He actually lived in No.5, nearest us, and it is praised for the beauty of its ceilings in Walter Ison's *The Georgian Buildings of Bristol* (reprinted 1978). Sadly these houses were pulled down to make way for flats in the 1950s.

In 1906 No. 5 was occupied by E. Colston Smethurst, No. 6, by Thomas Halse, a tailor, and No. 7, by Charles Hayward Baynton. [**34**]

Colston Villa, Horfield Road. Sandwiched between Colston's Almshouse to the south and Bengough's Almshouse to the north (the walls of which can just be seen to the right of the picture), this very pleasant-looking house, which is still with us today (minus its lovely garden), was in the tenancy of James Hugh Evans, who may well be the gentleman seen in his smoking-cap in the garden. Mr. Evans traded as Evans and Sons, masons and builders, and must have been around 72 when this picture was taken. The 1891 Census lists the occupants of the house as being, in addition to himself, Annie, his wife, Alfred, his son, Emily, his daughter, Jane Manning, his maiden aunt ('living on own means'), and Louisa Cox, a servant. Perhaps the two ladies in the picture are his wife and aunt. On the right hand corner of the house can just be seen a figure which might be Alfred, his son. [35]

No. 31 Horfield Road and Prior House, Robin Hood Lane. We are looking across Horfield Road and the grounds of Bengough's Almshouse (see photograph 10), towards No. 31 Horfield Road, which is almost hidden by trees, and Prior House, out of sight behind it. Running to the right of the houses is Robin Hood Lane, which climbs from Horfield Road to St. Michael's Hill, and still retains most of its original gas street-lamp; and indeed, now as then, connects with the Robin Hood public house at its top (St. Michael's Hill) end. The old door to Prior House, complete with pediment, can still be seen to this day in the wall on the southern side of the Horfield Road end of Robin Hood Lane.

The tenant of Prior House was Edward Pullen, a carpenter; that of No.31 Horfield Road is named in the 1906 Wright's Directory as Frederick Newton, secretary to the BMC Trustees. In their own copy of this directory, his name is crossed through, and in their schedule of their properties for the period, the tenant is named as H.W. Pearce.   [36]

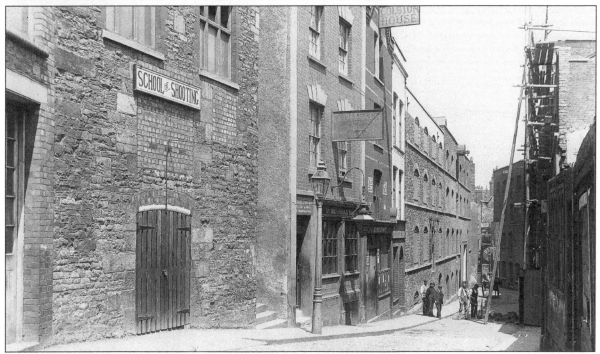

Host Street. Looking down Host Street from its Colston Hall end towards Christmas Street and the bottom of Christmas Steps. The BMC property here is a hay and chaff warehouse leased by the Bristol Tramways and Carriage Co. Ltd (just beyond the group of men to the left).

The warehouse remains in part. The building housing the School of Shooting is also still with us, as is the one next door on the other side of Zed Alley, the steps of which can be seen ascending between them towards Colston Street. The latter premises were then the St. Michael's Hotel, though now they are no longer a pub.

The shooting school represents an interesting phenomenon. They particularly flourished under the encouragement of Baden-Powell, who was concerned at the deficiencies in this skill shown by British recruits in the Boer War (which had not long ceased when these photographs were taken).   [37]

Jacob Street, Midland Railway Co. Stables. 'Stables and yard in the occupation of the Company (the Midland Railway Company); warehouse, office, foundry engineer's shop, storehouse and stable, in the occupation of their sub-tenants; with entrances from Unity Street', so states the BMC survey of the time. Note the wooden 'creeps' to convey the horses to the stalls on the upper floor. **[38]**

Jacob Street, Midland Railway Co. Stables. These premises ran from the south side of Jacob Street at its eastern (Trinity Hospital) end to Unity Street, and were just to the west of (i.e.. just behind) the site offered for let in photograph 47, and a very short distance up Midland Road from the Midland Railway Co.'s goods terminus, where no doubt the horses would have been employed, both for carting and shunting.

[39]

Jacob's Wells Road. 'Dwelling house, stables, cart houses, work-shops and yard adjoining the grounds of Queen Elizabeth's Hospital on the west side' says the BMC schedule of properties, 'tenant, executors of John Curnock'. The property is on the corner with Carr's (now John Carr's) Terrace, to the south west of Queen Elizabeth's Hospital, which can be seen here towering over the scene.

David Eveleigh in his *Bristol 1850 — 1919* (Sutton, 1996) has an interesting photograph taken from a similar angle a few years later, and states that the house just appearing at the right of the picture was built around 1894 and provided accommodation for the school's stable-keeper.

The two boys standing in front of the big doors are not QEH pupils, since they are not wearing the distinctive uniform; perhaps they are sons of the stable-keeper himself? **[40]**

Johnny Ball Lane, Albion Terrace. Johnny Ball Lane is a dog's leg of a thoroughfare running uphill from Narrow Lewin's Mead to Upper Maudlin Street, just above the Bristol Royal Infirmary. Its rather angular nature may be due to it having acted as the boundary between the land of the Grey Friars (or Franciscans) and that of St. Bartholomew's Hospital (later home to both Grammar School and QEH), and certainly a good part of its course marks the boundary between the parishes of St. Michael and St. James. Near the Upper Maudlin Street end was a burial ground, disused by this date, which the trustees of the BRI leased from the BMC at a peppercorn rent. This is the area of grass in the foreground (which survives to this day).

Beyond the railings is Albion Terrace which lay on the south west side of the burial ground and which the BMC owned. There were four houses, rented by Henry Charles Sprague (No.1), Daniel Organ (No.2), Wallace Charles Wills (No.3) and George Leeson (No.4). They seem to have been one up-one down, and crammed into a yard below the level of the burial ground, with only the one on the end, at the left side of the picture, possibly having a small garden (between it and the access-way to all the cottages off Johnny Ball Lane). At the back they abutted onto other buildings. Like most of the working class housing administered by the BMC they were let on a weekly tenure.   [41]

Johnny Ball Lane, BRI burial ground. The disused burial ground mentioned in the description of photograph 41, showing its well cared-for monument.

The burial ground was granted to the Infirmary in 1757 by Bristol Corporation for the interment of pauper patient fatalities. It was a small, rocky piece of land and soon became rather crowded. In 1770 it was quarried 'to make more room', but by 1815 the Council complained that the hospital authorities were not burying the dead deeply enough because they were putting several coffins on top of each other in one grave: 'in some instances the upper Coffin is scarcely under the surface of the earth'. It was decided to make the graves nine feet six inches deep, instead of nine feet. This would allow a bit of depth for earth on top of the sixth, and final, coffin in each grave. In this way another 1,924 bodies could me buried there! The ease of access to graves also meant that grave-robbers could quite conveniently ply their trade, providing illicit corpses for medical students to practice dissection upon. For instances of this practice, see Munroe-Smith, *A History of the Bristol Royal Infirmary*, pp. 208-9.

Interestingly, a plan in one of the City Council's plan books of property owned or administered by it, describes this area as the 'Soldiers' burial ground'. The plan is undated, but next to one of the 1740s, which might suggest that this was already a burial ground before the BRI took it over.

This was not the only burial ground in this kind of state in Bristol or in the country in general, and it, like so many others, was closed in the 1850s.   [42]

Jones's Lane, Redcliffe. Another dog's leg of a passage-way, running from the west side of Redcliffe Street, just below St. Mary Redcliffe Church, to the warehouses and wharves of Redcliffe Back. This picture looks as if it was taken looking back towards Redcliffe Street, which presumably is just behind the tall building with its back to us that fills the background. The BMC had two cottages, each with its own wash-house, in the lane: No.1 leased to Jane Bowley and No.2 to Henry Bridger, both rented on a weekly tenure. Perhaps this is Jane Bowley at the door of No.1. An insurance valuation for 1889, in the records of the BMC, indicates that originally there were three cottages here, and indeed one can see that there is a storey missing from the middle of the whitewashed cottages on the right. Perhaps it was demolished to give the occupants of the other two a little more space and to make the very cramped area less potentially insanitary. Sadly these lanes, like the dead-ended courts built in the gardens of the old burgage tenements, had tended, particularly in the nineteenth century, to be very squalid and unhealthy places.

Like Johnny Ball Lane, Jones's Lane ran past a burial ground: this time one used by the Society of Friends (Quakers), which was overlooked at its southern end by the shot tower on Redcliffe Hill (see photograph 73). Whilst the burial ground remains to this day, Jones's Lane had to make way for the approach to Redcliffe Bridge.   [43]

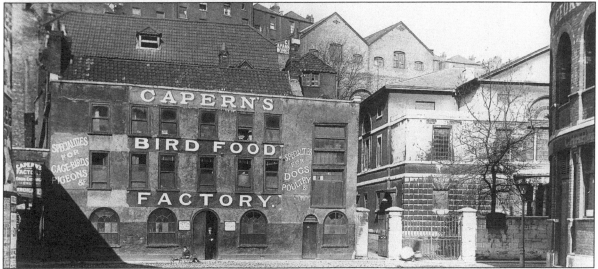

Lewin's Mead. An area which in the eighteenth century was considered fashionable and inhabited by merchants, some members of the Corporation, Lewin's Mead had dropped somewhat in status by 1906. Indeed in the mid nineteenth century it was the haunt of down-and-outs and the street children whose plight led Mary Carpenter to set up her reformatories in Kingswood and Park Row. By the turn of the twentieth century it was an industrial area, containing engineering works, printers, a brewery, a dry salter, and a timber merchant, amongst others. At the heart of it all, though, remained (as it does today) Lewin's Mead Unitarian Chapel, built in the late 1780s for the nonconformist great and good of the city. Half of its striking five-bay front and three-bay pediment can be seen to the right of the picture.

The BMC leased a portion of the chapel to the Feoffees of Lewin's Mead Meeting on a 500-year lease which had commenced in 1787. The lease also included the school behind. In addition the BMC also had a warehouse at the corner of Lewin's Mead and Johnny Ball Lane (just out of the picture to the left) which was leased by Edwin Mortimer Hodges and used as a bottle and cask store, possibly by Bristol Superaeration Co. But stealing the show in this photograph is 'Capern's Bird Food Factory', rented by Thomas Francis Mesmer Capern. This rather down-at-heel former sugar house, which still survives in an even more run-down state, seems to have received something of a 'make-over' in 1922, acquiring a rather ornate hood over its main door and a more gentrified, if bogus, Georgian air. The hood was a bone of contention between Capern's and the Council's Sanitary and Improvement Committee, who were reluctant to give permission for it since it protruded '24 inches beyond the statutory allowance'. Eventually honour was even when Capern's agreed to remove it whenever required to do so by the Committee. It is still in place at the present time.

The whole of this site backed onto Johnny Ball Lane (see photographs 41-2).   [44]

Narrow Lewin's Mead. We are looking along Narrow Lewin's Mead towards Lewin's Mead itself at 'workshops, warehouses and offices, with entrance from Christmas Street', as the BMC schedule of properties says. These are occupied by Burleigh Ltd., printers, lithographers, photoengravers, etc; producers, we must assume, of the *Western Counties Graphic, South Wales Graphic* and someone's *ABC Railway Guide.* Just beyond the premises, on the right of the picture, is the entrance to Johnny Ball Lane. [45]

Nos. 24-25 Mary-le-Port Street. A sunny day in the heart of the old city. Looking from the south side of Peter Street, across Dolphin Street and down Mary-le-Port Street. To the left can just be made out the railings at the entrance to St. Peter's Church and Hospital beyond. In the centre of the picture, on the corner of Dolphin Street and Mary-le-Port Street are the imposing premises of Mackenzie, Finlayson and Co., woollen merchants (Nos. 24 and 25 Mary-le-Port Street). Beyond, are a wood engraver, a window ticket writer, tailors' trimmings dealers, a carpet depot, woollen Manchester merchants, to name but a few and indeed only half of one street. It makes the old city's shopping centre seem somehow more vibrant than today's. [46]

the corner site, with its sense of dereliction and neglect, does look in desperate need of development.

In contrast to what is happening behind the hoardings, the scene in front has almost the vibrancy of a painting by L.S. Lowry (who was studying art in Manchester at the time the picture was taken): the hoardings themselves illustrate the Edwardian working-class style of life, with their adverts for household products (Colman's starch, Chef sauce), consumables (Westward Ho tobacco, Bass beer), and entertainment (Empire theatre — 'twice nightly', Evan Roberts' *Good Words* with a story entitled 'Queen of the Rushes'), mostly illustrated with a Victorian zest and good humoured

Midland Road/Unity Street. All human life seems to be here as people go about their business in front of the cluttered bill-posting stations on the corner of Unity Street (to the left) and Midland Road (to the right). These were leased by the BMC to the billposters Billing, Jarrett, Read, and Co. Ltd., of Excelsior House, Colston Street.

The picture is taken from the corner of Waterloo Road by St. Philip's Station (Midland Railway) and we are looking up Midland Road past the eastern side of Trinity Almshouses towards Old Market Street. The poster on the side of the house behind the hoardings proclaims 'To Be Let: Building Site, Warehouse and Manufactory, Frontages Midland Road/ Unity Street. Enquiries to the Bristol Municipal Charities', and indeed

innocence that was yet to be challenged by two world wars. This was a bustling working-class district close to the heart of Bristol's heavy industrial area. Midland Road was full of shops, pubs, refreshment rooms, pawn brokers, nonconformist chapels (Christian Brethren and Primitive Methodist) and had the parish church on it (Emmanuel). The Midland Railway had its goods station there and at the Upper Railway Wharf; eight or nine coal merchants operated. The streets around also teemed with industrial housing for the workers (men and women) in the mills and factories of St. Philip's. In the moment in time caught here we see men at work hauling timber, or pushing the ubiquitous hand cart, and women with children, most notably the lady with the pram. [47]

No. 1 Milk Street, the Plume of Feathers Inn. Looking from the Horsefair towards the corner of Barrs Street (to the left) and Milk Street (to the right). From here the size of Clarke's clothing manufactory can be appreciated (see photograph 49), and in the centre of the picture we have the Plume of Feathers, landlord, Richard Chapman. It was actually leased to Michael Clune, like several similar working-class public houses belonging to the

BMC. To the left of the Plume of Feathers in Barrs Street is William George Radford, saddle and harness maker, and indeed saddles can just be made out in the window. Just beyond Clarke's premises can be seen the facade of Milk Street Chapel (United Methodist Free Church).

(See photograph 14 for a view from Old King Street, which is off to the right on this picture.) [48]

Nos. 3, 5, 7, 9, & 11 Milk Street. Looking down the north side of Milk Street towards its junction with Barrs Street (to the right, just beyond the lamp post) and the Horsefair (straight on). To the right of the picture can be seen part of the enormous (and fairly new) premises of Robert Clarke and Co., wholesale clothiers, which extended to and included Nos. 6 and 7 Barrs Street. Next door to this is the hairdresser, William Frederick Taylor's, shop (No.5). His neighbour, at No. 3, is Thomas William Jones the fruiterer, whose tall baskets of produce can be seen outside the shop. All now under the north eastern corner of the modern Broadmead shopping centre. **[49]**

Nos. 34-35 Narrow Wine Street. We are looking down the southern side of Narrow Wine Street towards the corner of Church Lane (which led south, across the piazza of today's Castle Park, to Peter Street and St. Peter's Church). Nearest us, at No. 34, is the warehouse of G.E. Crabbe and Co., cycle and motor factors, (note that the top story is occupied by the Monarch Typewriter Co.); next door, on the corner, are the premises of Globe Express Ltd., general carriers, who, as Globe Parcel Express Ltd., also had a receiving office at 140 Whiteladies Road. G. E. Crabbe and Co. were also described as cycle manufacturers.

On the wall behind the man sweeping up is a wonderful poster provided by the London and South Western Railway, advertising Lyme Regis as a holiday destination; beyond this is a timetable for that particular railway company.

These properties would first have given way to Fairfax House, the department store, and then the Galleries shopping complex. **[50]**

No. 11 Nelson Street. The tenants were J.S. Fry and Sons Ltd., the chocolate and cocoa manufacturers, based at this time in the Union Street/Broadmead area. This warehouse was one of their half a dozen packing case depots. The premises also seem to have been occupied in part by H.H. & S. Budgett & Co. Ltd., wholesale grocers. However, the next year the building was set to become part of the modern age, when the tenancy was taken over as a garage by the Truscott Motor Repository.

We are looking from the Bridewell Street end of Nelson Street. Also visible is the Midland Railway receiving office and the premises of Allen, Davies and Co., wholesale stationers and printers, both at No. 9 Nelson Street.

These buildings have all since been swallowed up by the Magistrates' Court complex. [51]

Nos. 22, 24, 28 Nicholas Street. We are looking towards the north side of Nicholas Street. From right to left: the entrance to a passage which led to Shannon court and also gave access to, at No.22, Stubbs & Burt, anatomical boot-makers and above them, the offices of the Christchurch Meat Co. Ltd.; the entrance to Athenaeum chambers, which were offices occupied by C. & C. Thompson, architects and surveyors (successor to Josiah Thomas),and H.G. Pearson, quantity surveyor; No. 24, Edward Parsons and Co., seed merchants; and at No. 28, W. F. Bowman, accountant, and the premises of N.E. Methley, wine and spirit importers, and the Hawkesbury Wine Co. of New South Wales.

The cellar under No. 28 was used by the Bristol Liberal Club (which since 1889 had occupied the Athenaeum itself, which was hidden by these buildings), as the gates indicate. Above them, at No. 26 (not owned by the BMC) were the offices of Frank Jefferis, stock and share broker, F.W. Hunt, auctioneer and valuer, and Morgan & Co. (A. Hodge), law stationers.

Behind this sober facade, on 6 March 1906, the Liberal Club held a 'smoking concert' in the Athenaeum. Members were given a pianoforte solo, a violin solo, a banjo solo, and a comic song, amongst others. On 16 March, there was a billiard match between the Liberal Club and the Literary and Philosophic Club. **[52]**

Nos. 9,11,13 Old King Street. We are looking up the south western side of the street from its corner with Broadmead. At No. 9 we see the shoeing forge of Radford & Co.; next door at No. 11 are the premises of Charles Henry Thrush, cycle maker; and next door again, at No. 13, the Excelsior Electrical Works of Helps, Woodfin & Co., electrical engineers. To the left of the picture is the building occupied by Henry Jones, flour manufacturer ('Jones' patent flour towers above them all'), which stood at the corner with Broadmead, between which and the shoeing forge two veterinary surgeons, James M. Broad and Alexander Macadam, had their practices; and to the right we can just see a lady in a shop doorway: possibly Mrs Eliza Lawrance who operated as a wardrobe dealer at No. 15. Soon after this, Nos. 11 and 13 were being referred to jointly as a building site.

Old King Street led north west to Barrs Street (see photograph 14). It is now under Merchant Street in the Broadmead shopping centre. [53]

Nos. 29, 30 and 32 Old Market Street. Nearly ten-to-four in the afternoon, looking east along Old Market Street towards Alderman Stevens' Almshouse. The three BMC-owned properties are in the middle of the photograph: the Bunch of Grapes Inn (No. 29), with two gentlemen having a conversation in its doorway; the Don refreshment house (No. 30), its window boasting 'sausage and mash'; and just beyond the clock, Owen Brothers, grocers (No. 32). Also seen are, from left to right: the Bristol Paint Co.; the Empire Studio, advertising 12 'midget photos' for 4 old pence (the drawing of the crocodile invites, 'come and be snapped') and the premises of Robert Townsend, surgeon-dentist (both at No. 28); Mackay and Co., confectioners (at No. 30a, to the right of The Don); William Glass, watch maker (No. 31); and beyond the Owen Brothers' shop, the rather grand premises of George Scudamore and Co., grocers, who also had premises in nearby Wade Street, St. Jude's. The entrance to Alderman Stevens' Almshouse can just be seen on the extreme right, just beyond the news-boards of Elizabeth A. Cusson, newsagent.

This picture shows us a glimpse of long-vanished street-life. To the left, two men stand next to their hand-cart (containing onions), outside the Bunch of Grapes a horse-drawn cab waits, and further down the road, an advertising hoarding is being moved by hand-cart. A trail of horse dung down the middle of the road testifies to the most prevalent form of transport.

To give an idea of the scale of the buildings: whilst the public house remains today, it has been knocked through into the premises here occupied by The Don, to make one establishment. It is still not what might be called large. [54]

Nos. 46-50 Old Market Street. Looking down the north side of Old Market Street from Lawford's Gate, just above the junction of Old Market Street, Midland Road (on the left), Lawford Street (on the right) and West Street. The BMC-owned properties are in the middle of the photograph, being, from left to right: Amos Raselle, pawnbroker and jeweller (No. 46); John Smith Burgess, seedsman (No. 48); H. Adams, confectioner (No. 49); and clearly visible, Walter Gibbs, hatter, at No. 50 (on the corner with Lawford Street). There seem to have been two No. 50s in Old Market Street at this time: Gibbs' premises on the north of the street, and the Swift Beef Co. opposite, on the south side. Later Gibbs' shop became No. 49A (one assumes to avoid confusion). No. 47 is supposed to have been empty at this time, though a sign saying 'Ash & Co.' is visible above the premises. To the extreme right of the photograph, on the opposite corner of Lawford Street from Gibbs, is The Palace, wine and spirit vaults (still there today).

This shows us a crowded street scene, which like photograph 47 seems to be a microcosm of Edwardian life. A policeman stands at the centre of the crossroads as a wagon carrying timber passes him; ladies push prams and cycles are visible, as are other wagons further down Old Market Street; a group of boys loiter on the corner of Midland Road and West Street; a small boy pushes a hand cart up Lawford Street. The young girl with a parasol at the centre of the picture suggests that it is a hot day. [55]

Nos. 50-52 Old Market Street. Looking up the south side of Old Market street towards Lawford's Gate. On the far left is Trinity Hospital South and the junction with Midland Road. At No. 50, with Jacob Street between it and the almshouses, is the Swift Beef Co. Ltd.; next door lives a doctor, Charles W. Belfield M.D., surgeon; and next door to him, are the premises of John E. Allen, poulterer and game dealer. Each of these properties included a dwelling in addition to business premises, exemplifying the practice of an earlier age, when business and professional people not only often 'lived above the shop', but also a greater variety of those 'shops', meaning businesses of all scales and varieties, were mixed together in one small area. Nearest us, on the right of the picture are the Mason's Arms and, at No. 54, Henry Banwell, pork butcher (neither BMC tenants). [56]

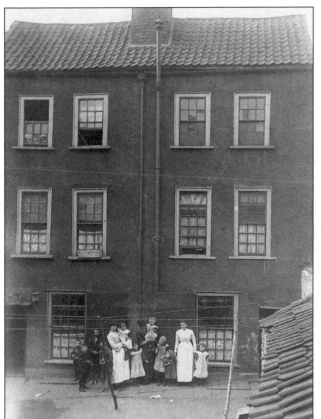

Old Market Street, Barcroft Place. Accessed via a narrow passageway on the north side of Old Market Street at its Lawford's Gate end, between Nelson and Sons the butchers and Raselle the pawnbroker (see photograph 55). Barcroft Place was a typical 'court': a group of five houses sharing a common wash-house, squashed into a yard behind the buildings on the street-line.

The tenants were Walter Edward Knight (No. 1), Alfred Povey (No. 2), Edward George Pickford (No. 3), George Alford (No. 4), and Daniel Tanner (No. 5). These need not necessarily have actually been the people living there. The families shown do not seem well-off, and the place seems strewn with litter and a little run-down, but it does not appear to be a particularly bad example of a court. The 1891 Census shows that, with one exception, the houses were lived in by one family each, the members of which all being employed, and the heads of household generally having skilled manual jobs. The little group to the left seem rather scruffier than the rest and at least two of the children seem to have bare feet — perhaps they have wandered in from elsewhere. Certainly two of the little girls in the middle seem to be watching them intently. Note, behind the two women in light-coloured dresses are shutters to cover the two ground floor windows.

The houses have now gone, but the courtyard survives as a car park to modern housing. [57]

Orchard Lane/Gaunt's Lane. A close up of the gateway seen from a distance in photograph 25. The roadway coming towards us is Gaunt's Lane and Orchard Lane goes off to the left, down to the Plymouth Brethren chapel on the corner with Orchard Street (see photographs 59 and 62). Just to the left is Sidney Berry's shoeing forge, and through the gateway, in Stratton's Yard, is St. Augustine's Hall, with some of the work force of Ford and Canning, bonded warehouse keepers, who leased this and the monolithic Protheroe's warehouse just to the left of where the photographer is standing.

The BMC considered St. Augustine's Hall to be on St. Augustine's Parade in their schedule of properties, since it could be accessed via a narrow passageway there, but for the purpose of loading and unloading it was obviously only possible to reach via Gaunt's Lane and this archway.

The yard beyond the archway has now been smartened up and the buildings re-developed as offices.

The BMC owned so much of this area because the Corporation of Bristol had granted the mansion house and orchard belonging to the thirteenth century monastic foundation known as Gaunt's Hospital, to Queen Elizabeth's Hospital (the City School) in 1590. The Corporation had obtained the Gaunt's Hospital estate at the Dissolution of the Monasteries. The school occupied the mansion (on the corner of Denmark Street and Unity Street, the site now occupied by the old Merchant Venturers' Technical College) and gradually the orchard was built on (hence 'Orchard' Street and Lane, and 'Gaunt's' Lane. [58]

Orchard Lane. We are looking down Orchard Lane towards Orchard Street. At the far end, on the corner, is the former Huguenot chapel. The properties in which the photographer is interested are the shoeing forge, smithy, stable and office of Sidney Berry, and Orchard House beyond. Perhaps Mr Berry is one of the figures standing outside the premises in the shaft of sunlight allowed by Hobbs' Lane opposite them. Orchard House was a dwelling which boasted a small van-house. The BMC also owned a workshop, a cottage (let to Ellen Kensalla) and a cellar in Orchard Lane. With the exception of the workshop, which was let on an annual basis, these properties were weekly tenancies, suggesting perhaps less prosperous tenants than many of those renting from the BMC.

[59]

Nos. 10-14 Orchard Street. Looking from the corner of Denmark Street at a row of houses extending from Denmark Avenue to Orchard Avenue, which were built in 1718. In 1906, as today, this street was considered to be a prime location for the professional classes to live and work. At No. 10 two civil engineers had their offices: Arthur Powell and Thomas Scott Scoones; at No.11 lived William John Tucker; at No. 12 were Henry William Wiltshire and John Walls; at No. 13 were the offices of the Crimean and Indian Mutiny Veterans' Association; and at No. 14 lived Mrs Sarah Ann Reeves. No. 10 also had its own caretaker, Frank Charles, and cellars leased to John Harvey and Sons Ltd, the wine merchants, whose premises were, and are to this day, in Denmark Street. (The BMC leased a number of cellars to Harveys, running under properties in Orchard and Unity Street.

A coal merchant makes a delivery and, at the end of the street, the Colston Hall can just be seen, dominating the skyline.

[60]

Nos. 15-19 Orchard Street. The continuation of Orchard Street from Orchard Avenue to its dead-end. Again built around 1718, this section of the street is wider than the other, because originally it was considered to be a square, and accordingly was named Orchard Square. At the time that this picture was taken, No. 15, nearest us, was empty, although later that year it would be leased by E. A. Harvey; at No. 16 was John Frederick Williams; at No. 17 was the Bristol Eye Infirmary; at No. 18, Samuel Martin and Son, builders, Edwin Martin, and A. Tambling, builder; and at No. 19, Edwin Hancock. At the end of the cul-de-sac can be seen the premises of Light Motors Ltd., and the backs of the buildings in Pipe Lane, with the Colston Hall peering over their roofs. [61]

for use as the Mayor's Chapel. The Corporation, so Latimer tells us, offered the displaced Huguenots this plot of land in Orchard Street at a nominal rent upon which to build their chapel, conveniently overlooking the fact that it actually didn't own the land but held it in trust as part of the estate of Queen Elizabeth's Hospital. The Huguenots stayed until 1825, by which time the congregation had dwindled so much that it was broken up. For a while it saw service as a medical library and then was taken by a congregation of Plymouth Brethren in 1856. The building was demolished just before World War II and its replacement now houses the offices of the Trustees of the Bristol Municipal Charities. It looks somewhat dilapidated in 1906, with its render falling off and its wall covered with the chalk graffiti of children's street games.

Nos. 20-24 Orchard Street and chapel. The set-back, south-eastern side of what was originally Orchard Square. Nearest us, on the corner with Orchard Lane, is Orchard Street Chapel, built by the Huguenot (French Protestant) congregation of St. Mark's church in 1727, when the Corporation took St. Mark's back again

The block of houses to the left of the chapel, built around 1722, were occupied by (from left to right): Arthur Tilbury Craker (No. 20); Sidney Cheetham (No. 21); Mrs James Collier (No. 23); and John James Tucker (No. 24).

[62]

Nos. 25-29 Orchard Street. The side opposite Nos. 10-14 Orchard Street, taken from the end of Unity Street. Nos. 25-26, furthest from us, were built around 1722; Nos. 27-29, like the majority of the street, around 1718.

At the end of the terrace furthest from us, were Miss Parsons and William Fryer, printer and bookbinder; next but one

contained Miss Josephine Mary Frazier, dressmaker; then, with its light over the doorway and the two gentlemen talking beneath it, the Sneyd Park Congregational Church Mission. The house on the corner with Denmark Street was known as Gaunt House, and was home to the Vigilance Association (Bristol and South Western). On its Denmark Street side, as can clearly be seen, A.

Nos. 2-4 Park Place, St. Michael's. The north-west side of Park Place, looking down towards St. Michael's Hill and Colston's Almshouse opposite. In the doorway of No. 4 are two ladies in starched aprons, one of whom perhaps is Mrs Emma Turner, the tenant, or perhaps they are domestic servants. At No.3 beyond lived Edward Nehemiah Bartley, and next again, at No.2, Mrs Howland. Right at the bottom, the shop-front of Frederick Ives, the grocer, can just be seen.

In the 1891 Census, taken 15 years before, a family of two adults and eleven children is recorded as living at No. 4; the head of the household being a french polisher at this time. No. 3 was occupied by a brickmaker's labourer with six children. The social status suggests, therefore, that the ladies in the picture are tenants and not servants.

The fact that those recorded in Wright's Bristol Directory for 1906 as living at Nos. 2 and 3 are not the same people to whom the BMC let the properties suggests that sub-letting of residential accommodation was allowed.

Neither these nor the houses in the picture that follows have survived, though the properties on each corner, facing St. Michael's Hill, are still there. The gentle, occasionally stepped, slope of Park Place itself remains as a means of access to the University.

[64]

Nos. 7-9 Park Place, St. Michael's. The south-east side of Park Place, looking down to St. Michael's Hill and Colston's Almshouse; just behind the houses is St. Michael's church. At No. 7, nearest us, lived Michael John Taylor, next door was William Cullen, and next again, James Edwin Price. All three were renting directly from the BMC.

One of the ladies from photograph 64 has now moved down the hill and is standing by the few steps that led to St. Michael's Hill. She still seems very interested in what the photographer is doing!

At No. 9, recorded as in the tenancy of James Price, was Sarah Jane Price, whom the admission register of Red Maids' School shows acting as guardian to her grand-daughter, Winifred Nellie Davis, at this time. Winifred was born not far away in Kingsdown in 1895 and was admitted to Red Maids in September 1905, when she was nine years old. She left in 1909, when only thirteen, the reason being given as 'removed by Governors'. Why she was removed is not recorded.

[65]

Nos. 7-9 Peter Street. The north-west side of Peter Street, directly opposite St. Peter's Church. Starting at the corner of Church Lane (see photograph 50), we see the Cash Boot Stores, followed by, at No. 8, Adams & Co., tobacconists, and Vosper, Paget & Co., pastry cooks and confectioners. The latter also boasts the Vosper Paget Cafe and Vegetarian Restaurant by means of a sign that can only be described as *Art Nouveau*.

[66]

Nos. 16-17 Peter Street. A little further along the street from the previous photograph, near the junction with Castle Street. Two ladies are just passing No.16 Peter Street, tenanted by Henry E.D. Marshall, hairdresser, and also housing (upstairs) the Bristol branch of the National Anti-Vaccination League (T. Gaylard, hon. sec.). Between the first and second floor windows is carved 'BMC 1887'. Mr. Marshall was of course a men's hairdresser, as the name of his business makes clear: 'Marshall's Hair Cutting and Shaving Saloon'. To the right, at No. 17, is E.C. James, pork butcher.

To the left of Marshall's is the Fox Inn (landlady Elizabeth Savage) with three likely lads lounging outside, and James A. White's Birmingham warehouse, an exotic emporium housed in Bristol Byzantine splendour. Neither of these properties belonged to the BMC. Peter Street ran alongside the north side of St. Peter's Church, from Dolphin Street to Castle Street. It was destroyed in the Blitz and today its site is the piazza opposite the Galleries shopping centre.

[67]

Portwall Lane. We are looking eastwards along Portwall Lane towards Temple Gate. The scene is the intersection of Thomas Street (on the left) and Phippen Street (on the right). The BMC owned buildings on the right, containing John Radford's marine stores (on the corner), the Redcliff oil and colour stores, the Argus Pressure Gauge Manufacturing Company, the Redcliffe Zinc Works, and Cooper Brothers, potato merchants. These have now given way to the landscaped area around Chatterton's birthplace.

On the left are the Chatterton Dining Rooms, boasting 'breakfasts, dinners, teas, and beds'. In Wright's 1906 directory this is listed as a 'coffee tavern' run by Henry King. Beyond are the premises of Albert Williams, a forage (i.e. animal feed) dealer. These have now been replaced by the large premises of a car dealer.

At this time the whole area, made up of the parishes of St.

Thomas, St. Mary Redcliffe, and Temple, all but surrounded by water, bisected by the Harbour Railway, and looking towards the joint stations of Temple Meads at its western end, was full of industry, both large and small. Even a relatively short street like Portwall Lane contained wholesale stationers and grocers, GWR stables, two pubs, a fish merchants, a newspaper office (Lloyds News), an ice store, and the wonderfully named 'Sweetmeat Automatic Delivery Company', in addition to the businesses already mentioned. The people who worked in the businesses also lived locally, as this picture testifies, with children and a dog mingling with busy workers.

Portwall Lane itself is now open on its southern side (the right hand section of the picture), being mainly used for car parking; and also cut through near its eastern end (furthest away here) by the thundering traffic of Temple Way.

[68]

Portwall Lane. The far end of the previous picture. We are here looking at the eastern most end of Portwall Lane, on its northern side, as it approaches Temple Gate and its intersection with Temple Street. The buildings in the picture were warehouses leased by C.S. Bailey and Co. Ltd. (probably the cutlers and ironmongers with extensive premises on Victoria Street), A.W. Ford and Co., wholesale stationers, and Samuel Appleby and Son, wholesale grocers, whose business premises were just round the corner in Temple Street. Shortly after this picture was taken Ford's took over Bailey's lease.

The one-storey building to the right of the picture is still with us, though it has lost its pediment and certainly seen better days.

The warehouse itself has gone, but it was sited where Redcliffe Way and Temple Way now meet, running from where Portwall Lane ends today, under the 'temporary' Redcliffe flyover, towards the back of the Grosvenor Hotel (whose chimney can just be seen on the photograph, rising above the end of the warehouse).

The graffiti is intriguing, tantalisingly telling us of '…that faster lover in…' and then subsiding into a seismographic chalk line trailing into the distance and Temple Street. Dragging a piece of chalk along the side of buildings seems to have been quite a popular bit of mischief at this time, as other photographs show. **[69]**

Redcliffe Back. Warehouses and an office at rear of Nos. 85 and 86 Redcliffe Street (see photograph 77), rented and used by James Selden Weymouth, the metal merchant, whose sign can just be seen above the two men in conversation to the left of the picture. Redcliffe Back also contained the premises of corn merchants, automobile engineers, pickle and sauce makers, and the Western Counties Agricultural Co-operative Association (to the right of Weymouth's premises) at this time. It had only a row of monumental mills and warehouses, punctuated by wharves, between it and the Floating Harbour. Note the youth of the workforce sitting on sacks in the doorway of the WCA warehouse. None of these buildings remain, their open sites being used for car parking; but just out of shot, to the right of the scene shown, the Western Counties Agricultural Co-operative Association's offices, built in 1897, still stand, alone in their narrow splendour. They can clearly be seen when approaching Redcliffe Bridge. **[70]**

No. 59 Redcliffe Hill. The Hope and Anchor Inn, which came with stables at the rear and the house adjoining (no. 63). The landlord was Pearce Organ, and Mrs Mary Taylor lived at No. 63, which seems to be part of the inn but has its own doorway. We are looking up the hill towards St. Mary Redcliffe church, which is flying what looks like the red ensign. Just outside the Hope and Anchor is a cabmen's shelter, presumably occupied, since a cab waits outside. The buildings to the left of the inn are: Robert Melhuish, greengrocer; Herbert Hillier, mineral water manufacturer; and, in the imposing building, Farnham Budgett, tea merchant.

Whilst one solitary old house now sits restored and alone on the corner with Colston Parade (just visible here between the church and the cabmen's shelter), the rest of this row have succumbed to Blitz and redevelopment, being replaced by offices. [71]

Nos. 92, 94, 96 Redcliffe Hill. The west side of Recliffe Hill, at the Bedminster Bridge end. At No. 92 is William Edward Poole, the baker; at No. 94, Charles E.H. Collard, the butcher, with his own slaughter-house on the premises, as was common; and at No. 96, Robert S. Cole, the plumber. Outside Mr. Poole's shop is his hand-cart, probably used for home deliveries. In a scene redolent of *The Ragged Trousered Philanthropist* both his premises and Mr. Collard's are being painted, perhaps at the expense of the landlord, the BMC. If this was the case, no doubt Mr. Cole's shop was either due the same treatment, or had already received it. Red-cliffe Hill was very much a place of shops and small businesses at this time.

The BMC's contractors for 'roofs, drains and outside painting' were S. Curnock and Son, of the Triangle, Clifton.

These shops were just to the south of Guinea Street (to the right of the picture), and have now vanished, as has the whole of this end of the hill, under multi-storey flats. [72]

Nos. 20, 26, 28 Redcliffe Hill. Opposite St. Mary Redcliffe church-yard. On the corner of Redcliffe Hill and Redcliffe Parade was the shot tower and warehouse of Sheldon, Bush and Patent Shot Company, manufacturer of shot and lead pipe.

In 1782 a local plumber, William Watts, patented his method for manufacturing shot. Until this point lead shot had been cast in moulds, but, (so he claimed), inspired by a dream in which he saw molten lead falling from the roof of a burning St. Mary Redcliffe church, Watts proceeded do drop molten lead from a height into cold water, thus creating near perfect pellets. Soon after, he built a tower on top of a late seventeenth century merchant's house opposite St. Mary Redcliffe, and, by also excavating the cellars, gained enough height to make his method practicable. Watts made quite a lot of money but lost most of it in building Windsor Terrace in Clifton (almost literally sinking it into the huge foundations of the house at the end of the terrace,

overlooking the Avon), and was forced to sell his business and patent. The Sheldon, Bush and Patent Shot Company took over the building in 1868 and remained there until the late 1960s, when it was demolished in order to widen Redcliffe Hill. This meant the sad loss of one of Bristol's oldest surviving brick-built buildings, and Watts' eccentric Gothic tower, built to remind Bristolians of Westminster Abbey. [73]

George Langford also rented a 'time wire' at No. 28. Next door can be seen the Ship Inn, landlord Walter Beacham, which had its own stable and coach-house; and beyond that, a few doors down at No. 20, the bootmaker, Harry Tyte. The premises on the other corner of Redcliffe Parade (not a BMC tenant) are 'The Supply Stores', proprietor W. Jennings, its windows full of tins stacked in traditional pyramids, and advertising 'easter cakes'.

It is now a grassy area incorporating the beer garden of a fairly modern pub.

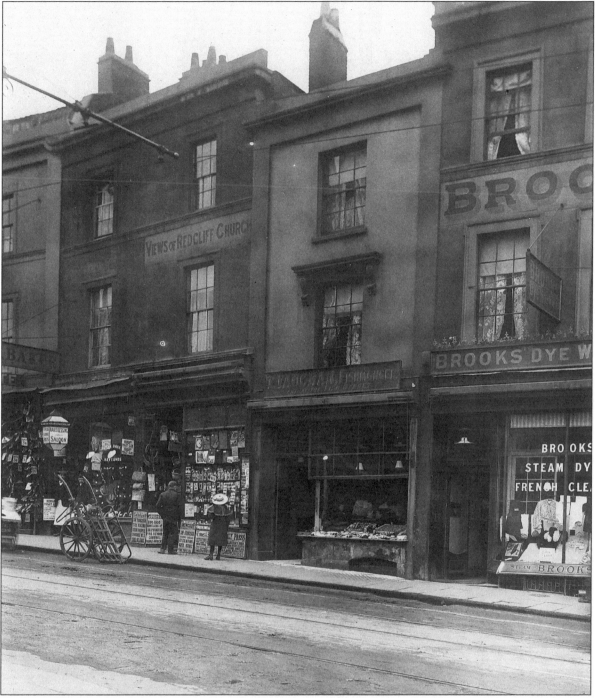

No. 14 Redcliffe Hill. A few doors down from Harry Tyte's boot shop (see photograph 73), we see the home and premises of Thomas Vaughan the fishmonger, with the traditional marble slab displaying the fish in the open air for customers. To the left (not a BMC property), is the stationery and fancy goods shop of Sidney P. Walter, boasting 'views of Redcliff Church' on its facade. Perhaps Mr. Walter added to his profits by allowing people upstairs to look out at St. Mary Redcliffe opposite, or perhaps (and this is more likely, given the contents of his window) he was just advertising prints and postcards. To the right of Vaughan's (again not a BMC property), is Brooks' Dye Works, later Brooks the dry cleaners.

The newspaper boards outside Walter's shop tell of the fires in San Francisco brought about by the earth-quake there. The *Daily Express* says: '250,000 Homeless at San Francisco — Fire Beyond Control — More Shock'; the *Bristol Mercury* mentions 5,000 dead in San Francisco, and proclaims 'Awful Scenes'; it also tells us that the Pope is ill. **[74]**

Nos. 1-3 Phippen Street. The corner of Redcliffe Street and Phippen Street, to the north of St. Mary Redcliffe, at 1 p.m., if the clock on Smith's premises is to be believed. These buildings stood roughly where the Redcliffe roundabout is today.

From left to right: Ernest Smith, jeweller and watch repairer; Edwin Robert Scoulding, furniture dealer; and William Day, greengrocer. A group of schoolboys (perhaps from Redcliffe School) take a lot of interest in a handcart, presumably from Scoulding's, loaded with furniture. With their facades plastered with advertisements these buildings seem to be acting as hoardings independent of the businesses actually occupying them.

These premises were listed with their Redcliffe Street holdings by the BMC; probably for convenience, given their proximity to the latter. [75]

Nos. 76-78 Redcliffe Street. Looking up the west side of Redcliffe Street towards Freshford Lane, Phippen Street just below us to the right. These buildings made way for the approach to Redcliffe Bridge. At No. 76 is James Mee, bootmaker, then William C. Hancock, confectioner, at No. 77, and Frederick A. Jenkins, florist and fruiterer, at No. 78. Between them and Freshford Lane are refreshment rooms (The Redcliffe Coffee Tavern) and yet another boot warehouse (not BMC properties). The rather grand premises on the far side of Freshford Lane are occupied by Albert E. Horder, tailor and outfitter, and next to him are the three golden balls of a pawn shop.

[76]

Nos. 83-87 Redcliffe Street. Starting at the pawn brokers seen in the distance on the last photograph. No. 83 is the double-fronted building in the centre of the picture, and houses T. Riordan and Co., provision merchants, Harry Gloster, carver and gilder, the Western Counties Agricultural Co-operative Association Ltd, and E. J. Hill and Co., cigar merchants. The building was huge, stretching all the way to Redcliffe Back behind (see photograph no. 70) and was probably, like so many of the buildings in this area, based on the layout of the original long, thin burgage plots, the sites of the houses and businesses of the medieval merchants. The following description of just Riordan and Co.'s part, from the BMC's schedule of properties, gives an idea of the size of the place: 'office (or shop) with rooms over, and counting house, warehouse, cellars and lofts in rear extending to Redcliffe Back, the whole forming southern portion of the premises; also warehouse on the northern side, with covered yard between; also an arched cellar under the premises...'.

At No. 84 is Samuel Nelson, butcher; at No. 85, George Howse, china and glass dealer; at No. 86, W. Shepherd and Co., grocers; at No. 87, Frederick Warry, tobacconist; at No. 87a, Walter Green, newsagent and stationer; and at No. 87b, William Henry Gould, furniture dealer. [77]

No. 107 Redcliffe Street. Further up the west side of Redcliffe Street. Described by the BMC as 'dwelling house, counting house, and undivided part of warehouses, extending to Redcliffe Back', these are the premises of William Burgess, public warehouseman, and include the lovely seventeenth century gabled facade, just to the right of the vacant pony and trap in the centre of the picture.

The imposing building to the right of the picture, a symbol of an industrial age dwarfing the much older buildings next to it, housed the cigarette works of W.D. and H.O. Wills.

It is 10.45 a.m. on a sunny Spring day, and a young girl in a very smart tam o' shanter and pinafore dress seems to look over her shoulder at the photographer.

All these buildings have given way to modern office developments. [78]

Bull Wharf, Redcliffe Street. Approaching the Bristol Bridge end of Redcliffe Street. A building extending to the Floating Harbour behind. It was used by the Severn and Canal Carrying Company, which received Severn trows (sailing barges) daily, carrying goods to and from Gloucester, Tewkesbury, Worcester, Stourport, Birmingham, Wolverhampton and elsewhere in the Midlands. The BMC owned a part of the building, their actual tenant being the wonderfully-named Miss Alice Heaven, who lived at the Ferns, Westbury Hill (there were a number of 'Heavens' living in Bristol at this time), and must have sub-let to the carrying company. Judging by the sign running across the top of the building, perhaps the Great Western Railway owned the rest.

Behind the group of bystanders is Mrs Mary Collins' dining rooms, providing food and drink for the workers: 'Large Coffee 1d.; Small Coffee d.; Small Tea H d.; Large Tea 1d.; Pot of Tea 1H d. Fresh Made; Rasher of Bacon H d.; Fried Egg 1d.'

The cart outside the building belonged to the Globe Express Ltd., carriers, of Narrow Wine Street. They were also BMC tenants and their premises can be seen on photograph 50. **[79]**

The Three Horse Shoes public house, Ropewalk, Narrow Weir. This was on the corner of Victoria Road and Haberfield Street and is now under the Haberfield multi-storey car park, where Bond Street meets Wellington Road. The Three Horse Shoes was just to the south west of St. Matthias Church (now gone). Looming behind it can be seen the vast premises of the Redcross Street Tannery, and perhaps we can assume that this was very much a pub frequented by the workers in the tannery, saw mill, foundry, and many other industrial occupants of this part of the city.

Mrs Sarah J. Wright was landlady, but not for much longer, since the records of the BMC show that the Three Horse Shoes

was soon after converted into two houses. The BMC also owned the timber yard to the left of the pub.

By the pub's main window, with its advertisements for Martell's brandy and other spirits, is a weighing-machine — somewhat incongruous outside a pub in a heavily industrialised area. Perhaps less surprising is a poster headed 'Rugby Football' and announcing the Easter fixtures.

The Three Horse Shoes was an extremely old establishment, and although alterations over the years hide it well in this photograph, was sixteenth century in origin. Slipped into the album from which this came is a Fred Little postcard with an artist's impression of how the building must have looked in its heyday. Both it and Ellsbridge Passage, with its entrance next to the man standing under the lamp to its right (see photographs 28-30), were reached by a bridge across the Frome. The building fell into disuse and C.F.W. Dening in his *Old Inns of Bristol* (3rd ed., 1944) says 'For many years the building has ceased to serve the purpose for which it was erected...the old Inn, which is in a bad state, has been condemned and awaits its fate of an early demolition'. **[80]**

Nos. 18, 20, 22, 24 Rosemary Street. Looking down the north side towards Water Street. The BMC properties are the four gabled, possibly seventeenth century, houses displaying a sign saying, 'To Be Let: The Whole of These Extensive Premises, having a Frontage of 57 Feet, a depth of 142 Feet, and an Area of 8437 Feet. Apply F.W. Newton Esq., Office of the Bristol Municipal Charities, St. Stephen Street'. These houses were the frontage to Broad's

Court (see photographs 82-3), which had probably been built in their gardens. The properties are bracketed by the premises of A. Deacon, packing case manufacturer, to the left, and the Merchant Venturers' Technical College workshops, to the right.

Rosemary Street ran along where the eastern half of Broadmead does today, giving access on its southern side to Quakers' Friars. **[81]**

Rosemary Street, Broad's Court. One of the many 'courts' still to be found in Bristol at the time: enclosed areas behind the street line, often the former gardens of the well-off merchants and tradesmen whose houses occupied the narrow burgage plots that made up the Medieval city. They were often cramped and insanitary, with many people crammed into small dark houses with poor accessibility. Broad's Court, however, seems fairly 'light' and airy. **[82]**

Rosemary Street, Broad's Court. A slightly different angle gives us another view of Broad's Court and one of its residents, emerging from his front-door. The BMC owned the five cottages in the court (as part of the premises advertised in photograph 81), all let on weekly tenancies. The tenants were: Thomas Dowling, Samuel Radford, Joseph Burt, Henry George Williams, and William Huxtable. Mr. Huxtable, at No. 6, was the only tenant recorded on the 1891 Census who was still there in 1906. He was 46 in 1891 and worked as a coach builder. He lived with his wife and grown-up daughter and son, the former being a chocolate maker (probably working at Fry's, just down the road), and the latter being a warehouseman. The households in Broad's Court do not seem to have been all that large, and the occupants were mainly skilled labourers. **[83]**

Rupert Street. We are looking westward along the north side of Rupert Street at the printer's workshops and paper warehouse of Allen, Davies and Co., paper merchants and manufacturing stationers, whose offices and salerooms were in Nelson Street nearby. The warehouse next door has obviously been used by J. S. Fry & Sons, whose factory was not far away in Union Street, but at the time that this picture was taken, it was to let.

These buildings occupy a line running parallel to, and just to the north of, the old city wall, which itself followed the course of the River Frome. This part of the street was created around 1880, the river having been closed over in 1867. [84]

Rupert Street. Looking from the corner of Christmas Street, (at the site of the city's Frome Gate), up Rupert Street towards Lewin's Mead. Here are BMC-owned printers' workshops and paper warehouse with offices, all leased by Ann Jenkins and Co., printers, stationers and account book makers (established 1840). The premises belonged partly to Queen Elizabeth's Hospital and partly to the Grammar School. Jenkins and Co. also leased the premises in photograph 84 from the BMC and sublet them to Allen, Davies and Co.

The posters stuck to the frontage nearest us are fascinating: On the top tier 'No more dead or weakly chickens', promises one, as long as you buy Pike and Tucker's biscuit and meat food. Pike and Tucker were based in Peter Street in the heart of the old city and Cathay in Redcliffe. Also advertised are Diadem self-raising flour, Spratts patent dog cakes, Lloyd's tea, Globe starch, and the billposters themselves, the aptly named Billing, Jarrett, Read and Co. of Colston Street nearby. The middle tier advertises theatre productions ('Mr. Forbes Robertson and Miss Gertrude Elliott and Company'), and the bottom one GWR excursions. The majority of the advertising relates to locally-based operations and enterprises.

The building to the right is the Oddfellows' Hall. [85]

No. 18 St. Augustine's Parade. No.18 is the building with *Canadian Pacific Railway* in large letters on its neo-classical pediment. The Canadian Pacific rented ground floor offices 'with lavatory and cellar under; including use of fixtures'. The Canada Life Assurance Company had two offices on the first floor, but at this point the rest of the building seems to have been empty, as the 'To Let' sign across the second floor indicates.

At this time the water of the Floating Harbour extended as far into the Tramways Centre as Smith & Co's furnishing warerooms, seen here near the middle of the picture, which gave way to the Hippodrome in 1912. Then, as today, the Centre, as it later came to be called, was just that for Bristolians — a focal point in a city that had sprawled dramatically, far beyond the old walls behind which it had largely been confined for most of its history; and beyond its traditional centre just above Bristol Bridge. The Centre was where many tram routes began and ended, at the commercial heart of the city.

If a reminder were needed that this was an age less brash than our own, one would only need to look at the advertisement outside 'Brightman's Boots': it announces a 'Resolute Clearance Sale'. [86]

Nos. 31, 33, 35, 37, 39, 41 St. Michael's Hill. These properties are on either side of Park Place (see photographs 64-5). We are looking down the SW side of St. Michael's Hill towards St. Michael's Church at the bottom. Below Park Place, at No. 35, was Edwin John Clarke, then next, at No. 33, was James Thomas Ballinger, and next again, at No. 31, Henry Owen. Above Park Place, we can see the shop front of the 'St. Michael's Stores', which were run by Frederick Ives, the grocer. Next up the hill at No. 39 was Mrs Davies, a widow, and next again, at No. 41, Miss Laura Matilda Smele, who was co-tenant with Walter Derrett.

St. Michael's Hill was, in the seventeenth and eighteenth centuries, a fashionable location for merchants wishing to get away from years of the rather too-cosy fashion of 'living over the shop' that had until that time been the norm for nearly all business people of whatever social status. The area was still largely rural then and seen as a healthy alternative to the fetid air of the cramped city. As the Revd Goldwin, master of the Grammar School, put it in his 'Poetical Description of Bristol' in 1712:

Here wealthy Cits discharged from worldly Cares
Conclude the downward Race of falling Years.
Here sickly Souls with broken Health repair
To suck the wholesome Drafts of healing Air. [87]

No. 28 (St.)Thomas Street, the Three Kings Inn. We are looking north towards Victoria Street, at the Three Kings Inn and the wine and spirit vaults of Malcolm Knee on the east side of Thomas Street, their seventeenth century facades hiding the goods receiving warehouse of the Midland Railway. Both licensed premises seem to be boarded up (and were, in fact, due for demolition). Nearest us are the premises of Price and Parker, provision merchants, with the van of the Iron and Marble Co. Ltd., whose premises were at No. 33 Victoria Street, but whose 'manufactory' was in Thomas Street itself.

Behind The old Three Kings, are hidden Burton's Almshouse, accessed by Long Row which ran between these ancient buildings and the warehouses of W.H. Smith and Son, wholesale newsagents. Disappearing out of the left of the picture, next to Smith's are the warehouses of Bolt Brothers, Manchester and Foreign warehousemen. St. Thomas Church is virtually opposite the latter.

Modern offices now occupy this site.   [89]

(Previous page): **St. Stephen's Street.** At the former Quay Head, up against the outside of the old city wall, we see 'Quay Head House', then the offices of the Trustees of the Bristol Municipal Charities themselves. It was designed in 1884 by Foster and Wood, and remains, in its red-brick splendour, to this day. To the left is the White Lion Hotel, landlady, Ellen Locke; to the right, illustrating that we are about to enter the commercial heart of the city, is a building crammed full of offices, including accountants, a building society, a land company, the Press Association, a produce broker, and, most apt of all, the Bristol Capitalists' Association. Then just to warn us that this is an era in which the districts of a city have not as yet become completely sanitized and compartmentalised, we also have a vinegar brewer.

Next to where until 1893 would have been the Floating Harbour, but which by this time was the entrance to the small park running down Colston Avenue that covered it, a gentleman takes a break sitting on the handles of his hand cart. Behind him, chained to the fence is a rather small water-trough, possibly for dogs. [88]

No. 119 (St.) Thomas Street, the Court Sampson Inn. It is not difficult to see that this is a very old part of Bristol. Here, it has lost some of its original prosperity and has been added-to and demolished, as the need arose, to accommodate the great variety of retail, wholesale and industrial activity, much of it at the less prestigious end of the scale, that has gone on here, particularly through the nineteenth century.

The Court Sampson Inn looks like an up-market seventeenth century house that has fallen on hard times. The doorway on its left hand side advertises John F. Cookman's shoeing forge and suggests that there is more going on behind the scenes than meets the eye. Like so many of the properties on Thomas and Redcliffe Streets at this time, the inn has behind it a long thin area, once its garden but now full of other buildings. A BMC survey of its properties describes the property thus: 'Court Sampson Tavern, with cottage, work-shop, shed and two warehouses.' All this behind one narrow facade. The inn and No. 120, the shop and warehouse next door to the right, were leased by the Bristol United Breweries Ltd. The landlord of the Court Sampson was Walter H. Gregory and the occupant of No. 120 was Henry R. Clake, rag and metal merchant. Next door, to the left (not a BMC tenant), was the shop of Eliza McKewan. **[90]**

Temple Back, the Jolly Sailor Inn. On the corner of Temple Back and Ash Lodge (see photographs 11-13), and now under the modern Temple Way, this seemingly run down old beer house was soon to be converted into just an ordinary dwelling house by Mr. Michael Clune of Tyndall's Park (a much more salubrious part of the city, up above the smoke and smell). Mr. Clune leased a number of pubs in working class areas of the city from the BMC, and in addition to this one, he was also about to change the use of the Three Horse Shoes in Ropewalk, St. Matthias (see photograph 80).

The landlady of the Jolly Sailor was Mrs Sarah Jane Pattison,

and perhaps the grinning gang standing to the side of the pub in Ash Lodge are her children. Perhaps they are pupils of the Temple Back Day Industrial Council School, next but one up the road! Temple Back and its surrounding streets and courts made up an area of fairly heavy industrialisation surrounded by the water of the Floating Harbour and New Cut, and bordering onto the Temple Meads goods yard to the west.

Next door to the pub was another BMC property, consisting of warehouses, workshops, stables, a dwelling house and offices. This was let to J.C. Wall and Co. Ltd, shipping and railway agents, who had a number of premises in the area. **[91]**

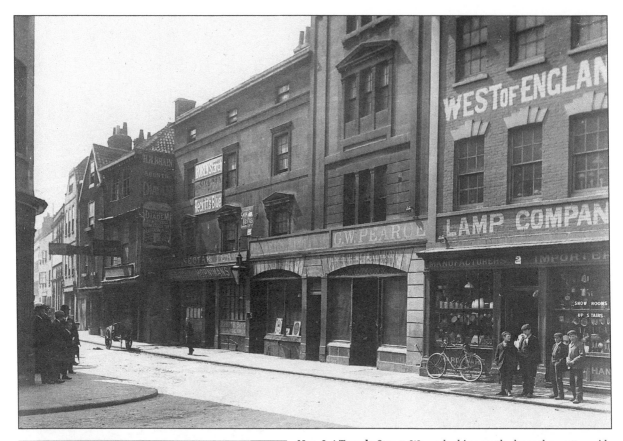

Nos. 2-4 Temple Street. We are looking south, down the western side of Temple Street North, from its corner with Philip Street. On the right can be seen The West of England Lamp Company at No.2. To the left of G.W. Pearce, sandwiched between the latter and Brain's wholesale grocery, is the wine and spirit shop of Olivers Ltd., or at least the entrance to their wholesale department. Olivers actually leased Nos. 1-5 from the BMC and obviously sub-let to the other traders. No.1, which is out of shot to the right, was occupied by John Stone.

These buildings have long gone, their sites now covered by modern developments. [92]

Nos. 3-5 Temple Street. This is the same part of the street as in photograph 92, but we are looking back towards the junction with Bath Street and Philip Street (where the photographer stood for the previous shot). The most prominent building in this picture is not a BMC property. It is the gabled seventeenth century facade of No. 6, with double bow-windowed shop front, housing John Hammett, the brass founder, and its adjunct, containing Robert Spiller, the carpenter, builder and shop fitter, which draws the eye. However the BMC owned the rest of the buildings in the photograph.

Property ownership in the old areas of the city must have been quite complex, given the amount of in-fill that went on behind the crumbling facades of its ancient street fronts. A BMC schedule of properties from about this time illustrates this in its description of No. 5 Temple Street: 'Warehouse and lofts adjoining No. 4...built over an entrance to property in Victoria Street not belonging to the Trustees, and over a passage forming a part of their own property'.

At Nos. 4 is the wholesale grocery business of Herbert Hill Brain and at No. 3 the wholesale stationery business of George W. Pearce. [93]

Nos. 104-105 Temple Street. Looking north west from Prince Eugene Lane, up Temple Street South, toward Victoria Street. We see to the right the premises of the United Yeast Company Ltd., based at No. 103, which does not seem to have been a BMC property. Nos. 104 and 105 next door, which were, consisted of a warehouse, stables, yard and hauling-way, and seem to have been shared between United Yeast and W. Baker, Son and Co., agricultural engineers. The rather run down-looking gabled seventeenth century house looks lost amongst the more recent and four-square warehouses. [94]

Appendix 1

Almshouses, Annuities and Gifts administered by the Bristol Municipal Charities, from the *Bristol Municipal Charities. Year Book 1905-1906*

Almshouse Charities.

Foster's Almshouse contains 28 inmates, viz., 5 men and 23 women, four women being appointed by the Lady Mayoress. The inmates are paid 7/- each weekly. Elections are generally held about a month after the vacancies are reported. The Trustees do not usually elect persons under 60 years of age. Applicants must have resided in the Parliamentary Borough of Bristol for not less than three years next preceding the time of their appointment, and must not have received poor law relief during that period.

Trinity Hospital contains 60 inmates, viz., on the north side 24, of whom 7 are men, and 17 women; and on the south side 36 inmates, of whom 4 are men, and 32 women. Weekly pay 7/- each. Qualifications, etc., as above.

Bengough's Almshouse contains 18 married couples and 2 single women. The weekly pay of a married couple is 10/-, and of a single person 7/-. One half the inmates are members of the Church of England and the other half Protestant Dissenters. Qualifications, etc., as above.
N.B. — A number of married couples, not exceeding 20 in all, may be admitted to one or more of the Almshouses.

Pensions. — After providing for the maintenance of the Almshouses, the surplus income of these Charities is applied in Out-Pensions of 8/-per week to single persons, and 9/- per week to married men, being poor persons of good character, not less than 50 years of age, who shall have resided in the Parliamentary Borough of Bristol for the time being for not less than three years next preceding the time of their appointment; have not during that period received poor law relief; and are unable, by reason of age, ill-health, accident, or infirmity, to maintain themselves by their own exertions.

Annuities and Annual Grants.

Sion Hospital Pensions — The Trustees nominate a number not exceeding four Men and four Women to pensions of the annual value of £36 for poor and impotent men or women so reduced in strength as not to be able to work, being inhabitants of Bristol and above the age of 50 years, and who have not been in the receipt of parochial (other than medical) relief within twelve months next preceding the time of election. When a vacancy occurs, the Trustees of Sion Hospital, London, notify the same to the Secretary (Bristol Municipal Charities), and thereupon two or more candidates are nominated for election. From the persons so nominated the election is made by the Sion Hospital Trustees. In case of failure to recommend candidates within three months after notice, the Trustees of Sion Hospital are empowered to fill the vacancy by the appointment of a person duly qualified, without restriction as to locality.
N.B.-This Pension is granted for a term of three years in the first instance, but may be prolonged for a further period of not more than three years at each prolongation.

Hannah Ludlow's Charity. — Annuities of £30 to Widows or Single Women, natives of

Bristol, and above the age of 50 years, who have been well educated and brought up and lived respectably and are of irreproachable character, but have become reduced in their circumstances, and have not been for the greater part of their lives domestic servants. There are 18 annuitants on the list, who are paid quarterly in advance. (Mr. Joseph Storrs Fry has the right of nomination of one annuitant).

Annuities and Annual Grants.

Margaret Edgar's Charity. — One annuity of £35 to a Single Woman, a native of Bristol, and above the age of 50 years, having qualifications similar to those requisite in the case of applicants for Hannah Ludlow's Charity.

The Edward Phillips Trust. — Annual Gifts of £30 to Gentlewomen, being Widows or Single Women, of the age of 55 and upwards; natives of, or having been resident for 10 years at least immediately preceding the date of application for the Charity, in the Municipal Borough of Bristol; who are in reduced circumstances, of irreproachable character, and who have been well educated and brought up.

The Edward Phillips Trust. — Annual Grants of £20 to Widows in reduced circumstances resident at the date of application within the Municipal Boundaries for the time being of the City of Bristol, having at the time of election a child or children under the age of 15 years: tenable during the pleasure of the Trustees, and only during widowhood, and generally only whilst a child under the age of 17 years is dependant on the recipient, although special circumstances will be considered. There are 10 widows on the list, who are paid quarterly in advance.

Bonville's (Housekeeper) Charity. — Annual Grants to poor *Housekeepers* over 50 years of age, living in the ancient city, and not in receipt of poor-law relief, who are of good character, and, when health admits, regularly attend some place of Divine worship twice on every Lord's Day. Widows and Single Women are to be preferred. There are five recipients of £21 each, 15 of £10 10/-, and 50 of £5 5/-. Elections to fill vacancies take place in February and August. The recipients are not annuitants, but are re-elected annually on the third Friday in January.

Annuities and Annual Grants.

Bonville's (Lodger) Charity. — Annual Grants to poor *Lodgers,* who are qualified as above, of £13. Vacancies are filled by elections in March and September. In this case also the recipients, not being annuitants, are re-elected on the last Friday in February or the first in March. There are 24 recipients at the present time.

The Edward Phillips Trust. — Annual Gifts of £7 15/- each to poor *Householders* of the age of 50 years and upwards, resident within the Municipal Boundaries for the time being of the City of Bristol. (The recipients of Bonville's Gift of £5 5/- to Housekeepers are alone eligible to receive these gifts).

Annual Gifts of £2 10/- to poor *Householders* qualified as above. (The recipients of Bonville's Gift of £10 10/- to Housekeepers are alone eligible to receive these gifts).

Merlott's Charity. — Annuities of £10 for poor persons above the age of 50 years, living in any part of Great Britain, who, having been "stone blind" for at least three years, are not receiving parochial alms, nor are common beggars, nor are already entitled to any estate, annuity, salary, pension or income for life to the amount of £20 a year. The vacancies (if any) are filled about January and July. There are 47 annuitants on the list, who are paid half-yearly in advance.

Annuities and Annual Grants.

Gist's Charity. — Annuities of £18 4/- each to three poor Men and of £15 12/- each to three poor Women; such poor men and women being over 50 years of age, natives of the ancient City of Bristol, who have never received poor-law relief nor alms from any public charity. Preference is given to persons who have been in better circumstances than the ordinary poor.

Edmund Lane's Charity. — Two Annual Grants of £15 to poor Tradesmen or Tradeswomen of good character, resident in the City of Bristol for the time being. In default of Tradesmen or Trades-women, persons who have ceased to carry on a trade within a period of twelve months are eligible.

Marriage Portions.

Dr. White's Gift of not more than £10 each to not exceeding four young Women on marriage is bestowed on the second Friday in January. Petitioners must have lived in service five years at least in the same family, or have steadily pursued for so long a period some other honest means of gaining a livelihood. Those applicants are preferred who have for some years been depositors in a savings' bank. Application must be made and the grant obtained before marriage.

Lying-in-Gifts

Whitson's and Ann Thurston's Charities. — 50 gifts of £1 are bestowed on as many Women in child-bed, residing in the Parliamentary Borough of Bristol. Application must be made before confinement. These gifts are apportioned monthly.

Whitson's Charity. — 20 Gifts of £1 are in the bestowal of the Lady Mayoress to Women living in the ancient city and otherwise qualified as above.

Lying-in-Gifts

Peloquin's £1 10/- Gift to 52 poor Lying-in Women, who are wives of Freemen. These gifts are in the nomination of the Lady Mayoress.

Haberfield's 25/-

Lady Haberfield's Charity. — *This* gift of £1 5/- is bestowed on the Friday before the 27th of December in every year on 10 poor Married Women (whose husbands are living) not receiving poor law relief.

E. Ludlow's £5.

Elizabeth Ludlow's Gift. — This gift of £5 is granted on the second Friday in February to five Widows or Widowed Daughters of Freemen, living in the ancient city. The gratuity is not, as a rule, given two years following to the same person.

Bibles.

Dr. Sloper's Gift. — For Bibles to be distributed amongst the poor in the Municipal Borough of Bristol. The Trustees have a printed form addressed to the Secretary directing that a Bible be given to the bearer thereof. Income £20.

Kitchen's "Poor Kindred" and Miscellaneous Gifts.

Kitchen's Charity. — Grants of £3 at Lady Day and £3 at Michaelmas, are made annually to the Alderman's poor kindred. No person can receive the gift oftener than once in three years. Small grants are made to "distressed citizens" from this Charity by a special vote of the Board.

Miscellaneous Gifts

The Edward Phillips Trust. — A sum of £50 is appropriated annually for the relief of deserving needy persons resident within the Municipal Boundaries for the time being of the City of Bristol, and for other Charitable Gifts in the discretion of the Trustees.

**Christmas and
other Gifts.**

Peloquin's Gift of £1 1/- to 20 poor Widows and Single Women, and 10 poor Men in the parish of St. Stephen, nominated annually by the Minister and Churchwardens of the parish.

Peloquin's Gift of £6 6/- to Freemen, or Widows or Daughters of Freemen, housekeepers in the ancient city, not receiving poor-law relief or keeping alehouses. This gift cannot be obtained by the same person oftener than once in three years.

Whitson's Gift of £1 to 104 Householders in the ancient city.

Whitson's Gift of 10/- to 52 poor Widows residing in the ancient city.

Holbin's Gift of 10/- to nine poor people in St. Thomas's parish, is distributed by No.1 Gift Committee.

Fuller's Gift of 10/- to the Poor of SS Philip and Jacob (In) is distributed by No. 7 Gift Committee. Annually £12.

Elton's Gift of 4/- to the poor of St. John's is appropriated annually. The Rector furnishes a list of the names, which is subject to approval by the Trustees. It is given on or about the 11th September. Annually £2.

Elton's Gift of 8/- each to five poor Householders of the parish of Saint Werburgh is distributed annually by No. 8 Gift Committee.

**Christmas and
other Gifts.**

Chester's Gift of 10/- *and* 5/-. — To seven inmates of St. John's Almshouse 10/- each, and to 18 poor Parishioners of St. John's 5/- each. The names of the latter are furnished by the Rector.

G. Harrington's Gift of 10/-. — This gift is distributed on the nomination of the Churchwardens of the several parishes, to the number apportioned to them, among Free Burgesses and Housekeepers of the ancient city. The forms are sent to the Churchwardens on Christmas Eve. Annually £27.

Jackson's Gift of 4/-. — This gift to 44 Householders in the ancient city, being Freemen or Widows of Freemen, is distributed by the Corporation, and paid at this office.

Kitchen's Gift of 10/-. — This gift, to 52 poor House-holders, is distributed and paid in the same manner as the foregoing.

Appendix 2

PROPERTIES PICTURED, ARRANGED BY THE CHARITIES WHICH OWNED THEM

Bristol Grammar School

Bristol Grammar School	Photo 1
Nos. 27, 29, 31 Berkeley Place, Clifton	Photo 17
No. 1 Christmas Steps (jointly with QEH)	Photo 20
Nos. 17 & 19 Christmas Street (jointly with QEH)	Photo 22
Host Street, warehouse (jointly with Whitson and Foster)	Photo 37
Johnny Ball Lane, Albion Terrace	Photo 41
Johnny Ball Lane, BRI Burial Ground	Photo 42
Lewin's Mead, seed warehouse and portion of chapel	Photo 44
Narrow Lewin's Mead, workshops, warehouses and offices (jointly with QEH)	Photo 45
Nos. 29-30 Old Market Street	Photo 54
Rupert Street, printer's workshops and paper warehouse: Allen, Davies & Co. (jointly with QEH)	Photo 84
Rupert Street, printer's workshops and paper warehouse: Jenkins & Co. (jointly with QEH)	Photo 85

Queen Elizabeth's Hospital

Queen Elizabeth's Hospital	Photo 2
Nos. 9-10 Upper Berkeley Place	Photo 18
No. 1 Christmas Steps (jointly with BGS)	Photo 20
Nos. 17 & 19 Christmas Street (jointly with BGS)	Photo 22
Christmas Street, Willway's Dye Works	Photo 23
Denmark Street, Protheroe's Warehouse	Photos 25-6
Frogmore Street, Denmark Avenue, offices and workshops	Photo 31
Nos. 22-30 Frogmore Street	Photo 32
Nos. 32 & 40 Frogmore Street	Photo 33
Jacob's Wells Road, QEH stable-keeper's premises	Photo 40
Narrow Lewin's Mead, workshops, warehouses and offices (jointly with BGS)	Photo 45
Orchard Lane, forge, etc.	Photos 58-9
Nos. 10-14 Orchard Street	Photo 60
Nos. 15-19 Orchard Street	Photo 61

Nos. 20-24 Orchard Street	Photo 62
Nos. 25-29 Orchard Street	Photo 63
No. 26 Redcliffe Hill	Photo 73
Rupert Street, printer's workshop's and paper warehouse:	
Allen, Davies & Co. (jointly with BGS)	Photo 84
Rupert Street, printer's workshop's and paper warehouse:	
Jenkins & Co. (jointly with BGS)	Photo 85
Nos. 2-4 Temple Street	Photo 92
Nos. 3-5 Temple Street	Photo 93
Nos. 104-5 Temple Street	Photo 94

Foster

Foster's Almshouse	Photo 8
Nos. 9-11 Christmas Steps	Photo 21
Host Street, warehouse (jointly with BGS and Whitson)	Photo 37
Nos. 34-5 Narrow Wine Street	Photo 50
Nos. 2-4 Park Place, St. Michael's	Photo 64
Nos. 7-9 Park Place, St. Michael's	Photo 65
Nos. 7-9 Peter Street	Photo 66
Nos. 16-17 Peter Street	Photo 67
Portwall Lane, warehouse	Photo 69
Bull Wharf	Photo 79
Nos. 31, 33, 35, 37, 39, 41 St. Michael's Hill	Photo 87
No. 28 (St.) Thomas Street, the *Three Kings* Inn	Photo 89

Whitson

Red Maids' School	Photo 3
Ash Lodge, Temple	Photos 11-13
No. 49 Corn Street	Photo 24
Host Street, warehouse (jointly with BGS and Foster)	Photo 37
Jacob Street, Midland Railway Co. stables (jointly with Trinity)	Photos 38-9
Nos. 22, 24, 28 Nicholas Street	Photo 52
Portwall Lane, oil and colour works, etc.	Photo 68
Temple Back, the *Jolly Sailor* Inn	Photo 91

Trinity

Trinity Hospital North	Photo 4
Trinity Hospital South	Photos 5-7
Alderman Stevens' Almshouse (site of)	Photo 9
Nos. 1-5 Barrs Street	Photo 14
Nos. 8-12 Barrs Street	Photo 15
Nos. 13-15 Barrs Street	Photo 16
No. 42 Broadmead	Photo 19

Jacob Street, Midland Railway Co. stables (jointly with Whitson)   Photos 38-9
Midland Road/ Unity Street, building site, etc.   Photo 47
No. 1 Milk Street, the *Plume of Feathers* Inn   Photo 48
Nos. 3, 5, 7, 9 & 11 Milk Street   Photo 49
No. 11 Nelson Street   Photo 51
Nos. 9, 11, 13 Old king Street   Photo 53
No. 32 Old Market Street   Photo 54
Nos. 46-50 Old Market Street   Photo 55
Nos. 50-2 Old Market Street   Photo 56
Old Market Street, Barcroft Place   Photo 57
Nos. 18, 20, 22, 24 Rosemary Street   Photo 81
Rosemary Street, Broad's Court   Photos 82-3
St. Stephen's Street, Quay Head House   Photo 88
No. 119 Thomas Street, the *Court Sampson* Inn   Photo 90

Owen

Nos. 25-31 Ellbroad Street   Photo 27
Ellbroad Street, Ellsbridge Passage   Photos 28-30
Nos. 5-7 Guinea Street   Photo 34
Jones's Lane, Redcliffe   Photo 43
Nos. 24-25 Mary-le-Port Street   Photo 46
Redcliffe Back, warehouse etc.   Photo 70
No. 59 Redcliffe Street, the *Hope and Anchor* Inn   Photo 71
Nos. 92, 94, 96 Redcliffe Hill   Photo 72
Nos. 20 & 28 Redcliffe Hill   Photo 73
No. 14 Redcliffe Hill   Photo 74
Redcliffe Street, Nos. 1-3 Phippen Street   Photo 75
Nos. 76-8 Redcliffe Street   Photo 76
Nos. 83-7 Redcliffe Street   Photo 77
No. 107 Redcliffe Street   Photo 78
Ropewalk, Narrow Weir, the *Three Horse Shoes*   Photo 80

Bengough

Bengough's Almshouse   Photo 10
Horfield Road, Colston Villa   Photo 35
No. 31 Horfield Road and Prior House   Photo 36

Gist and Peloquin

No. 18 St. Augustine's Parade (jointly with Bonville)   Photo 86

Bonville

Orchard Lane/ Gaunt's Lane, St. Augustine's Hall etc.   Photo 58

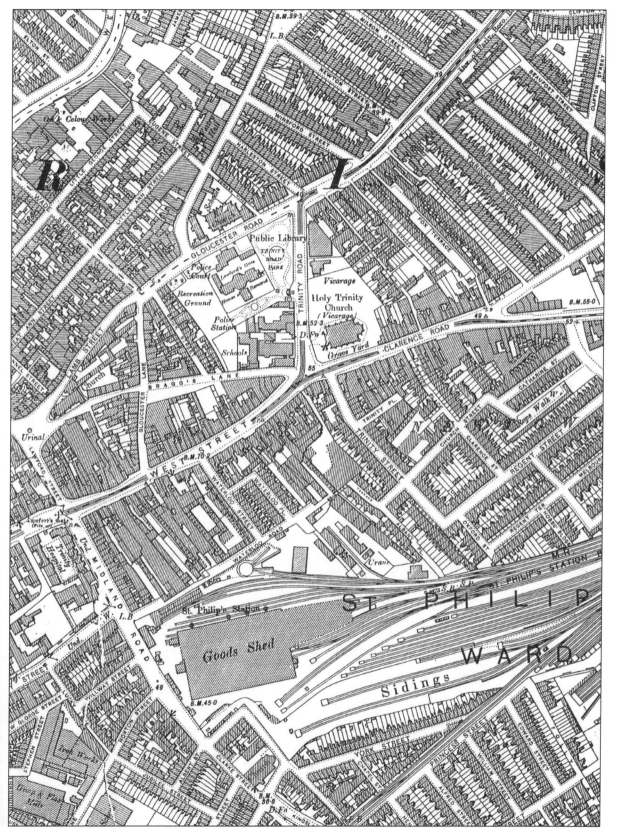

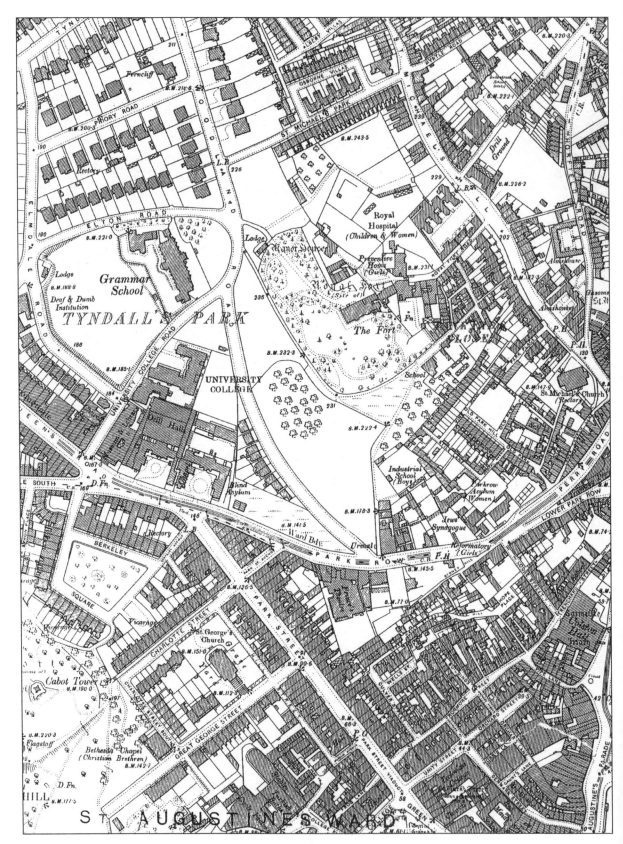

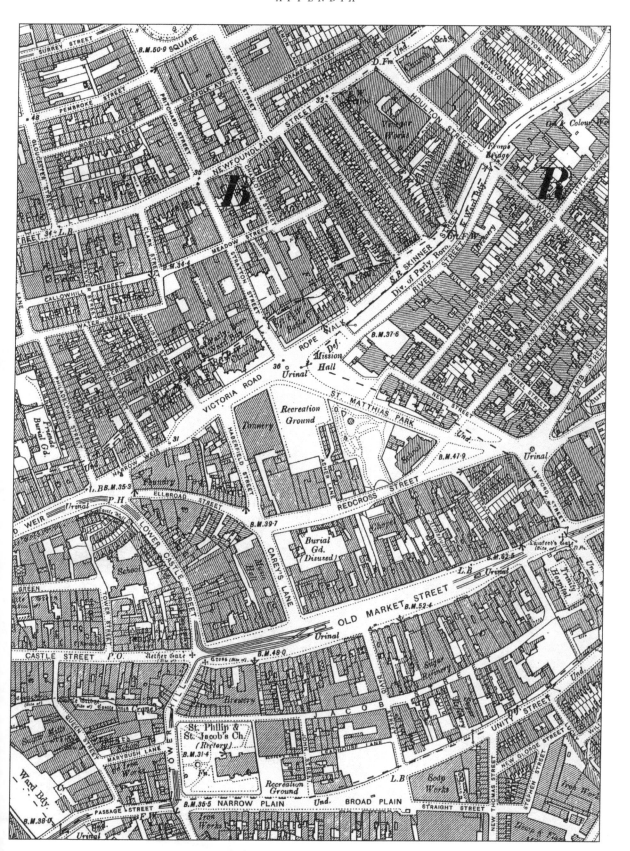

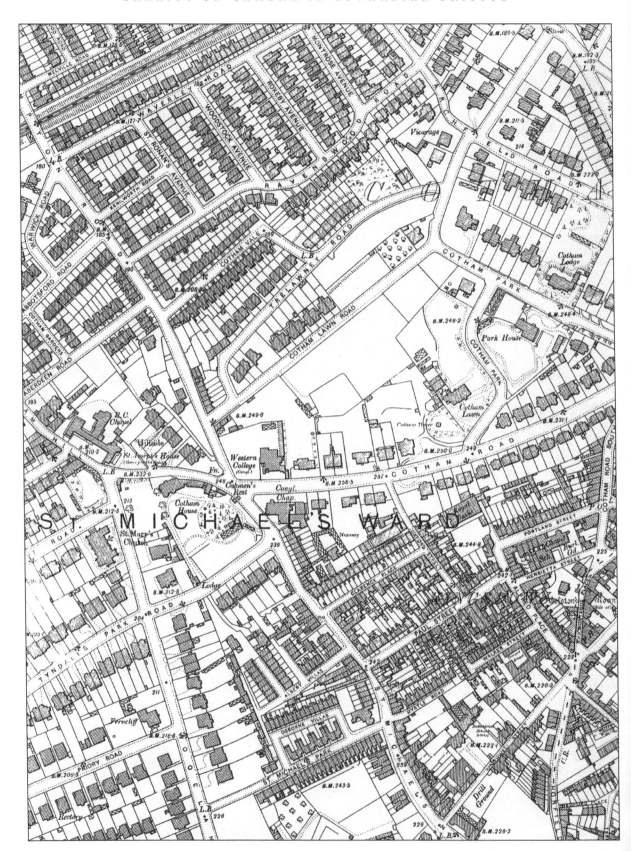

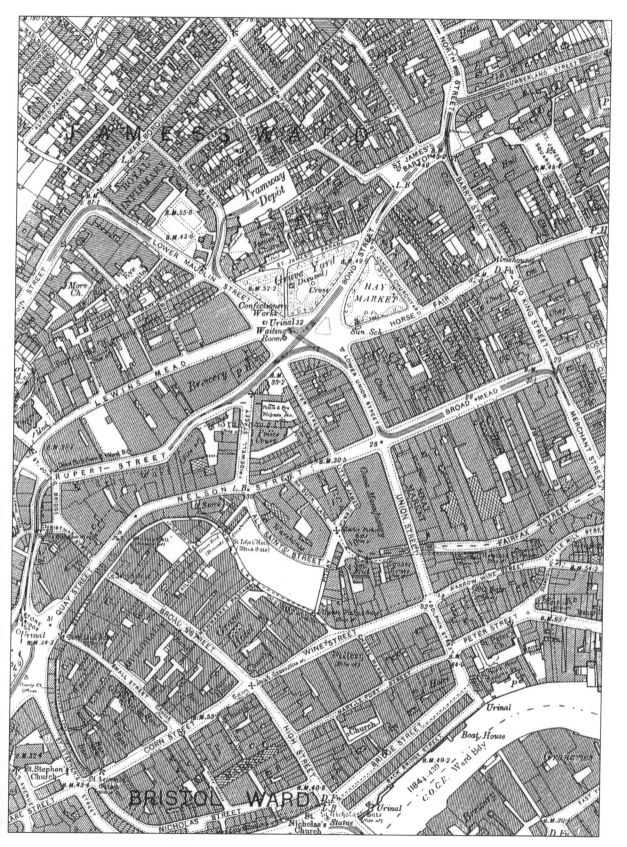

Bibliography

Since many books in this bibliography are out of print, the place of publication is not given save in circumstances where it might be confusing for readers wishing to follow up references; books on local history not published in their locality, for example.

Background

A good up-to-date book for studying late nineteenth and early twentieth century British history is Jose Harris, *Private Lives, Public Spirit: Britain 1870-1914,* 1994 in the Penguin Social History of Britain series. Other useful publications are: Simon Nowell-Smith, ed., *Edwardian England 1901-1914*, 1964. It contains a series of articles of which Asa Briggs, *The Political Scene*, pp. 44-101; Arthur J. Taylor, The *Economy*, pp. 105-38 and Margharita Laski, *Domestic Life*, pp.141-212 are the most relevant. Robert Cecil, *Life in Edwardian England*, 1969; Samuel Hynes, *The Edwardian Turn of Mind*, 1968; Ronald Pearsall, *Edwardian Life and Leisure*, 1973 and Rebecca West *1900*, 1982 are also good as is H.J. Dyos ed., *The Study of Urban History*, 1968 and W. Ashworth, *The Genesis of Modern British Town Planning*, 1954 (see especially pp 72-77).

Photographs

The number of books containing local history photographs are immeasurable. Examples which give an analysis of how photographs can be interpreted include: Shirley Baker, *Street Photographs: Manchester and Salford*, Newcastle-on-Tyne, 1989; H.D. Gower, *The Camera as Historian; A Handbook to Photographic Record Work for Survey or Record Societies*, 1916; Benny Green, *The Streets of London: Moments in Time from the Albums of Charles White and London Transport*, 1983 and Kieran Hickey, *Light of other Days, Irish Life at the Turn of the Century*, London, 1973. See also Raphael Samuel, *Theatres of Memory*, 1994, especially pp. 315-49 for an analysis of photography, its use and interpretation, particularly in the heritage industry and David Eveleigh, *Bristol 1850-1919*, 1996.

Bristol's History

Publications relating to specific aspects are presented within each chapter. The best book to read for background information is H.E. Meller, *Leisure and the Changing City, 1870-1914*, 1976, which is exclusively about Bristol and covers more issues than the title suggests. However, there is no one publication that gives an inclusive coverage of the city's history for our period. A good article is B.W.E. Alford's, *The economic development of Bristol in the nineteenth century: an enigma?* in *Essays in Bristol and Gloucestershire History,* edited by Patrick McGrath and John Cannon, 1976. For other articles, see also C.M. MacInnes and W.F.Whittard eds., *Bristol and its Adjoining Counties*, 1955; the *Victoria County History: County of Gloucestershire*, Vol ii, London, 1907 and Madge Dresser and Philip Ollerenshaw, eds., *The Making of Modern Bristol*, 1996

The Year 1906
Contemporary publications on and including Bristol

J. W. Arrowsmith, *Dictionary of Bristol*, second edition,1906 which is a mine of information, and is the best source for studying the city at this time.

S. A. Barnett, *The Ideal City*, n.d.

Board of Trade Enquiry into Working Class Rents, Housing and Retail Prices, 1908.

A. Cooke, *Bristol Hovels, The Report of the Bristol Housing Reform Committee, October 1907*

W. L. Dowding, *The Story of Bristol: A Brief History for Young Citizens*, 1906

Stanley Hutton, *Bristol and its Famous Associations*, 1907

John Latimer, *The Annals of Bristol in the Nineteenth Century*, 1893 edition

Lesser Columbus (Lawrence Cowen), *Greater Bristol*, London, 1893

George Frederick Stone, *Bristol As It Was — And As It Is. A Record of Fifty Years' Progress*. Reprinted, with additions, from the *Bristol Evening News* 1908-1909 (1909)

Secondary sources

D.J. Carter, *The Social and Political Influences of the Bristol Churches 1830-1914*, Unpublished M. A. thesis, University of Bristol, 1971

W.J. Daunton, *House and Home in the Victorian City: Working Class Housing 1850-1914*, 1983

Madge Dresser, *People's Housing in Bristol 1870-1939* in Bristol Broadsides, *Bristol's Other History (1840-1940)*, 1983

N.A. Ferguson, *Working Class Housing in Bristol and Nottingham 1868-1919*, Unpublished Ph.D. thesis, University of Oregon, 1971

J.H.S. Kent, *The Role of Religion in the Cultural Structure of the Later Victorian City, Transactions of the Royal Historical Society*, 1973 pp. 153-73.

H.A. Shannon and E. Grebenik, *Population of Bristol*, 1943

Charity

General

Norman Alvey, *From Chantry to Oxfam: A short history of charity and charity legislation*, 1995

Jonathon Barry and Colin Jones, eds., *Medecine and Charity Before the Welfare State*, 1991

F.M.L. Thompson ed., *The Cambridge Social History of Britain 1750-1850*; see vol. 3, *Social Agencies and Institutions*, 1990

Phillis Cunningham and Catherine Lucas, *Charity costumes of children, scholars, almsfolk, pensioners*, 1978

Kevin Grady, *The records of the Charity Commissioners as a source for urban history*, Urban History Yearbook, 1982, pp. 312-7

Robert Humphreys, *Scientific Charity in Victorian London: claims and achievement of the Charity Organisation Society, 1869-1890*, 1993

Robert Humphreys, *Bygone Charity — Myths and Realities*, London School of Economics Working paper no. 23/94, 1994

James Jamieson, *The Public Charities and Their Abuses*, 1880

C.L. Mowat, *The Charity Organisation Society 1869-1913, Its Ideas and Works*, 1961

Bristol

Bristol Municipal Charities: Their History And Constitution With Details Of The Charities Administered By The Trustees, 1974

City of Bristol: Charities Under the Management of the Municipal Trustees Inspector's Report, 1871

Ronald Cleeves, *Mission of Mercy*, 1979

Martin Gorsky, *Charity, mutuality and philanthropy, 1800-70*, Unpublished Ph.D. thesis, University of Bristol, 1995

T.J. Manchee, *Bristol Charities*, 2 vols., 1831

F. H. Towill, *Bristol Charities Past and Present*, in C.M. MacInnes and W.F. Whittard eds., *Bristol and its Adjoining Counties*, 1955, pp. 293-304

W. Leighton, *Endowed Charity in Bristol and Gloucestershire* in *Transactions of the Bristol and Gloucestershire Archaeological Society*, vol. 67, 1946-1948, pp. 1-20

Walter A. Sampson, *The Almshouses of Bristol* in *Transactions of the Bristol and Gloucestershire Archaeological Society*, vol. 32, 1909, pp. 84-107

Children

General

Pamela Horn, *The Victorian and Edwardian Schoolchild*, 1989

Stephen Humphries, *'Hurrah for England': Schooling and the Working Class in Bristol, 1870-1914*, Southern History, vol. 1, 1979 pp. 171-208

Stephen Humphries, *Hooligans or Rebels? An Oral History of Working-Class Childhood and Youth 1889-1939*, 1981

Stephen Humphries, *Radical Childhood (1889-1979)* in Bristol Broadsides, *Bristol's Other History (1840-1940)*, 1983

Bristol

F.W.E. Bowen, *Queen Elizabeth's Hospital Bristol: the City School*, 1971

C.P. Hill, *The History of the Bristol Grammar School*, revised edition, 1988

Walter A. Sampson, *History of Queen Elizabeth's Hospital*, 1910

Walter Adam Sampson, *A History of the Red Maids' School, Bristol, 1634-1908*, 1924 (completed edition)

Jean Vanes, *Apparelled in Red: the History of the Red Maids School*, 1984

Roger Wilson, *Bristol's Schools*, in C.M. MacInnes and W.F. Whittard eds., *Bristol and its Adjoining Counties*, 1955, pp. 311-22

There are also the series recordings making up the *Bristol People's Oral History Project* which are in the Bristol Central Reference Library. The collection covers a host of social issues affecting people who lived in or near the centre of the city at the beginning of the century. Transcripts for a good number of recordings have been undertaken.

The Elderly

Ian Archer, Spencer Jordan and Keith Ramsey, *Abstract of Bristol Historical Statistics. Part 1. Poor Law Statistics 1835-1948*, University of the West of England, 1997

Helen Bosanquet, *Poor Law Report*, 1909

Carl Chinn, *Poverty amidst prosperity: The urban poor in England, 1834-1914*, 1995

C.F.G. Masterman, *The Condition of the People*, 1909

Moira Martin, *Managing the Poor: The Administration of Poor Relief in Bristol in the Nineteenth and Twentieth Centuries* in M. Dresser and P. Ollerenshaw, eds., *The Making of Modern Bristol*, 1996, pp. 156-80

Report of the Committee To Inquire Into The Condition Of The Bristol Poor, 1884 (Edited by Rev. S.A. Walrond, vicar of St Lawrence Jury, London)

ND - #0135 - 270225 - C0 - 246/189/6 - PB - 9781780915159 - Gloss Lamination